D0492800

HIGHLAND
LIBRARIES

WITHDRAWN

Owls of Britain
and Europe

Owls of Britain and Europe

A. A. Wardhaugh

HIGHLAND
REGIONAL
LIBRARY

S.83 12380

598.97094

HIGHLAND
LIBRARIES

WITHDRAWN

BLANDFORD PRESS
Poole   Dorset

First published in the U.K. 1983 by Blandford
Press, Link House, West Street, Poole, Dorset,
BH15 1LL.

Copyright © 1983 Blandford Books Ltd.

Distributed in the United States by Sterling
Publishing Co., Inc., 2 Park Avenue, New York,
N.Y. 10016.

ISBN 0 7137 1260 0

All rights reserved. No part of this book may be
reproduced or transmitted in any form or by any
means, electronic or mechanical, including
photocopying, recording or any information storage
and retrieval system, without permission in writing
from the Publisher.

Typeset by August Filmsetting, Warrington, Cheshire.
Printed and bound in Great Britain by
Biddles Ltd, Guildford and King's Lynn.

Contents

For Benjamin

Introduction

It is two a.m. on a mild autumn night. For seemingly no reason one wakes and drifts half asleep, lying in the darkness, safe, warm and comfortable in bed. The night is silent and still. But then a tawny owl hoots softly in the distance and a multitude of images come tumbling into the mind. At first a tingle of gladness in knowing that life in the natural world is going on out there in the dark, in all its fascinating complexity. Then thankfulness at having been able to sense just a little fragment of it. The owl hoots again. Thoughts of its soft plumage and wide eyes provide comfort and a feeling of peace, yet its gaze is somehow chilling. After a longer pause it hoots a third time and one feels a desire to scramble out of bed and follow it. We are missing a great adventure, the mystery and magic of life in the night. There is a slight twist in the pit of the stomach. Why? Gradually the images merge and sleep overtakes again.

Why do owls arouse such a diversity of feelings in us? Only a little thought is needed in order to provide at least some of the answers. No doubt it is as predators that owls arouse feelings of dislike, repulsion and fear. Their nocturnal habit adds the supernatural aspect, perhaps compounding the feeling of fear. The ability to fly so silently and to see in the dark is an eerie combination.

Around these basic truths grew the folklore image of the owl as an omen of ill and herald of death, an image perhaps stimulated in part by the tendency of some species to inhabit ruins and little-used buildings. In addition, the nocturnal skrieks, chatters and barks of the tawny owl and the scream of the barn owl do nothing to allay such superstitions. This is an image which has a surprisingly long history, for a Sumerian tablet of about 2300 to 2000 B.C. depicts Lilith the goddess of death with two lions and two owls. In the first century A.D., Pliny the Elder wrote, 'when it appears it foretells nothing but evil and . . . is more to be dreaded than any other bird . . . whenever it shows itself in cities or at all by daylight it prognosticates dire misfortunes.' Of a comparatively more recent date is Shakespeare's *Julius Caesar* in which the murder is preceded by the statement:

> And yesterday the bird of night did sit
> Even at noonday, upon the market place,
> Hooting and shrieking.

Lastly, the scientific name given to Tengmalm's owl is *Aegolius funereus*, literally meaning 'ill-boding owl'.

In sharp contrast to this superstition is the association between owls and wisdom. Interestingly, this too has a long history, for some of the coins of ancient Athens bear an image of Athene, the goddess of wisdom, with a little owl (*Athene noctua*). In the tales of King Arthur, Merlin is described as having an owl upon his shoulder as a symbol of wisdom. And of course there is the owl of children's story books, wise and nearly always benevolent.

No doubt the key to our present ambivalent attitude toward owls is in our memories from childhood days. Here is the soft and cuddly toy owl. The main features of an owl's appearance beg for such a caricature; upright posture, big, round, forward pointing eyes, cheek-like facial discs, a relatively small nose-like beak and of course the ear tufts as an optional, extrovert addition. This image of the owl completely transcends that of the malevolent predator. The eagle in particular makes an interesting comparison. Lacking the above features, its image has become more that of nobility and wisdom. Among the mammals, the fox and the wolf remain the sly, crafty, cowardly and bad, and the bear had a smaller jump to make from the bumbling omnivore to the cuddly teddy.

With such an air of mystery and romance about them, it could be forgivable to think that the true facts about owls may be somewhat bland and mundane by comparison. But the real owls are truly fascinating birds. What other group of animals has asymmetric ears and tubular eyes, eyes that may be up to one hundred times more sensitive than our own in dim light? There are so many questions to be answered. How are these aerial night-time predators related to the rest of the birds? What are their origins in pre-history? There are five common owl species in the British Isles yet there are up to twice this number in some other parts of northern Europe. Why is this so? On the other hand why is there not just one species of owl, a 'super-owl' that ousted all the others

Tawny owl at home in suburbia

during the long course of evolution simply because it was the 'best' owl?

This book is an attempt to answer some of these questions and to provide descriptions of the 13 owl species of Britain and northern Europe. Yet it must be remembered that these are only a small proportion of the world's 135 or so species of owl, for the majority are tropical in distribution. For the British bird watcher the species of continental Europe are fascinating in their own right, ranging in size from the pygmy owl, little bigger than a house sparrow, to the 680-mm-long eagle owl, a species that has been known to take prey as large as roe deer. Some familiarity with these European birds also provides an insight into how the British owls fit into the more diverse natural communities of other geographical regions.

Just what constitutes a British owl depends in any case upon the definition employed. There are six owl species which are breeding birds in the British Isles: the barn owl, the tawny owl, the long-eared and short-eared owls, the little owl and the snowy owl. Of these, the little owl was introduced by man in the 1890s and the snowy owl, formerly an occasional visitor to Britain, first nested on the Shetland Islands in 1967. In addition there are a further four species on the British list which are very rare vagrants from the rest of Europe and North America. Perhaps some of these could have become resident in Britain after the last Ice Age but for the formation of the North Sea and the English Channel which act as effective barriers to colonization. A century or so after the introduction of the little owl the possibilities for further artificial introductions are interesting. Tengmalm's owl for example would perhaps not be too out of place in our coniferous plantations and no doubt many bird watchers would regard it as a welcome addition to the British fauna.

Lastly, the final chapter of this book offers a few practical suggestions on how to observe and study owls for those who would see and know the birds for themselves: a family of tawny owls, two adults and three well-grown young all peering down from varying heights around the trunk of a beech, seemingly basking amid the early morning sunshine and brilliant green leaves; a barn owl quartering Norfolk fields at seven p.m. in mid July, attempting to provide enough food for a growing family hidden away in the attic of a derelict cottage; a party of short-eared owls, winter nomads, drifting over rough pasture as snow begins to fall. In the end, perhaps, it is simple memories such as these that make the owls infinitely attractive and somehow very special for a great many people.

1 The origin of owls and their place among the birds

Before considering the origin of owls in pre-history it is necessary to have some understanding of the classification of present day species; that is, the place of owls among the birds. Classification of living organisms is useful because it provides a means of summing up what we know about them. By grouping plants and animals on the basis of their fundamental similarities we can imply a great deal about a particular group simply through its name. For example when talking about birds, the class Aves, we are indirectly describing all the features of that group: a backbone, warm blood, feathers and a host of other common features. The same holds good for any taxonomic (i.e. classificatory) group. The natural classification has a further advantage in that all the scientific names used are internationally recognized. For example the barn owl, which has a range that extends through five continents, has a great many common names in numerous languages but just a single, universally accepted scientific name, *Tyto alba*.

The birds make up one class of the chordate phylum (animals with a dorsal nerve cord or spinal cord and certain other features in common), a phylum being one of the major divisions of the animal kingdom (Figure 1). Classes of animals are in turn divided into orders; the bird class contains some 27 orders, the owls (the order Strigiformes) being one of these. The chief characteristics of owls are a consequence of their position in nature as nocturnal predators. They have the hooked bill and sharp talons of all birds of prey and in addition very large, forward pointing eyes which are highly sensitive in the dark and allow a wide field of binocular vision. But perhaps the most distinctive features are the facial discs or 'cheeks'. These structures are in fact associated with hearing and appear to funnel sounds into the ears. A detailed discussion of these and the other features of the Strigiformes will be found in the next chapter. As can be seen from Figure 1, the order is subdivided into two families, the Tytonidae which includes the barn owls and

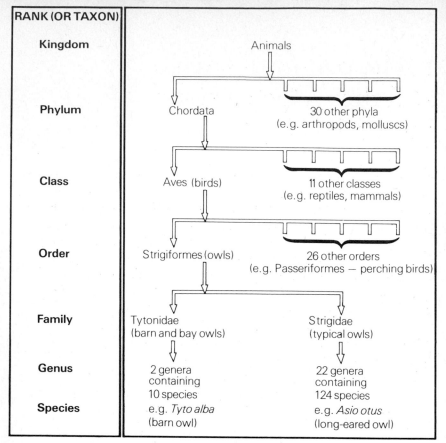

RANK (OR TAXON)	
Kingdom	Animals
Phylum	Chordata / 30 other phyla (e.g. arthropods, molluscs)
Class	Aves (birds) / 11 other classes (e.g. reptiles, mammals)
Order	Strigiformes (owls) / 26 other orders (e.g. Passeriformes — perching birds)
Family	Tytonidae (barn and bay owls) / Strigidae (typical owls)
Genus	2 genera containing 10 species / 22 genera containing 124 species
Species	e.g. *Tyto alba* (barn owl) / e.g. *Asio otus* (long-eared owl)

Fig 1. The classification of owls

bay owls, and the Strigidae which contains all other owls. Finally, the two families are each divided into a number of genera, closely similar species or types of owl being placed within the same genus. Thus for example the long-eared and short-eared owls are both placed within the genus *Asio*, the scientific name for the long-eared owl being *Asio otus* and that for the short-eared owl being *Asio flammeus*.

In Britain there are six resident species of owl and a full list of the British and European species is given in Table 1. It is of interest to note that all but one of the European species belong to the family Strigidae, the lone exception being the barn owl which belongs to the smaller Tytonidae family.

There is a further, very important aspect of classification worthy of mention and that is the implied relationship between organisms

TABLE 1 THE OWLS OF BRITAIN AND EUROPE

Family	Genus	Species	Common Name	Status
Tytonidae	Tyto	T. alba	Barn owl	Resident in Britain
Strigidae	Nyctea	N. scandiaca	Snowy owl	Resident in Britain
	Bubo	B. bubo	Eagle owl	Vagrant in Britain
	Asio	A. otus	Long-eared owl	Resident in Britain
	Asio	A. flammeus	Short-eared owl	Resident in Britain
	Asio	A. capensis	African marsh owl	Not recorded in Britain*
	Otus	O. scops	Scops owl	Vagrant in Britain
	Aegolius	A. funereus	Tengmalm's owl	Vagrant in Britain
	Athene	A. noctua	Little owl	Resident in Britain
	Glaucidium	G. passerinum	Pygmy owl	Not recorded in Britain
	Surnia	S. ulula	Hawk owl	Vagrant in Britain
	Strix	S. aluco	Tawny owl	Resident in Britain
	Strix	S. uralensis	Ural owl	Not recorded in Britain
	Strix	S. nebulosa	Great grey owl	Not recorded in Britain

* Rare vagrant from Africa in Spain and Portugal.

placed within each taxonomic group. Indeed, as the natural classification has been progressively developed, one of the prime aims has been to group together organisms on the basis of those similarities which are thought to be the result of relationship or common descent. Ideally every taxonomic group should contain organisms with a single common ancestral species. In the case of the owls the assumption is that the order Strigiformes arose from one single stock or species of bird and that this trunk of the evolutionary tree of the owls has two limbs, one line of descent leading to the barn owls (Tytonidae) and the other to the typical owls (Strigidae). Where are these ancestral stocks now? The answer is that they have long since become extinct, superseded by a succession of species and ultimately those of the present day. It is not inaccurate to say that classification is an indication of evolutionary relationships but perhaps it is more true to state that one of the aims in classifying is to reflect evolutionary pathways. The accuracy of that reflection rests upon the evidence and knowledge so far obtained about the evolution of the group of animals or plants in question.

As with all vertebrate animals, a good deal of what we know about the origin and evolution of the owls has resulted from the study of fossils. Unfortunately fossilized remains of owls are relatively uncommon. This is because most owls rarely live near, or frequent, river deltas and coastal areas where fossils readily form. Here the carcasses of animals reaching the water are quickly buried in sediment. Then over a long period of time the sediment and any remains preserved within it are petrified by the great pressure of further material laid above. Later, geological uplift of the rock may result in fossils becoming exposed either naturally at cliff faces or artificially by man, for example in quarries.

Unlikely though such a sequence of events may seem for any birds or other animals with inland habitats, a number of fossil owls have been discovered and in fact over 40 extinct species have been described. About 25 of these are members of the Strigidae and have been found within rocks up to about 40 million years old (i.e. from the Upper Eocene period onwards). A further dozen or so fossil species belong to the Tytonidae and are of an age up to 25 million years (from the Lower Miocene period onwards). Thirdly there are fossils of a few primitive species, mostly from Wyoming in North

America, which are undoubtedly owls but are considered to be quite different from those of the present day. For this reason they have been put in a family of their own, the Protostrigidae, a name meaning 'first owls' as some of these birds lived around 50 million years ago during the Eocene period. They may have been in existence even earlier than this and possibly constituted the trunk of the owl evolutionary tree. In their appearance and habits it is likely that these birds were quite distinctly owls, nocturnal or maybe crepuscular birds of prey with quite well developed facial discs.

In recent years there have come to light the most ancient fossil remains of owls currently known. These are a species from rocks of the Palaeocene in Colorado and two species from the Upper Cretaceous found in Romania, one of the latter having been named *Bradycneme draculae*. It has been suggested that both the Romanian species should be placed in a fourth owl family (the Brady-cnemidae), but it should be stressed that all three species are known only from a few fossilized leg bones (principally the tarso-metatarsi).

It will be apparent from the above that relatively little is known about the evolution of owls. There are several reasons for this, not least being that fossil birds are something of a side-line and not associated with the evolutionary history of man. Compared with the fossilized bones of mammals, those of birds are more difficult to identify, there often being only very slight variations between closely related groups. Furthermore, as has already been stated, for inland species the chances of fossilization taking place are slight.

Nevertheless, from the knowledge so far gained it has been suggested that the owls originated from other birds at some time late in the Cretaceous period, perhaps somewhere between 90 and 65 million years ago. This was at the close of the age of the dinosaurs when the earth was populated with plants and animals very different from those of today and long before the emergence of man. But the ultimate origin of owls, the ancestral stock which gave rise to the whole order is quite unknown. As for the species making up the Protostrigidae, they were probably all extinct by about 40 million years ago, replaced by forms successively more like those we know today. The genera *Bubo*, *Strix* and *Tyto* (see Table 1) probably all originated between 25 and 12 million years

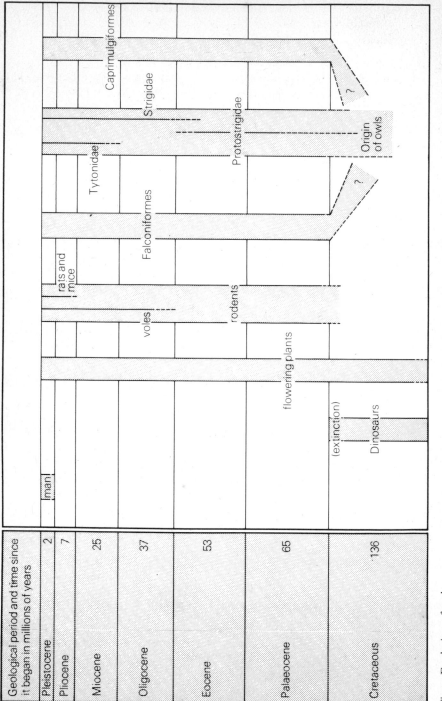

Fig 2. Evolution of owls

ago during the Miocene period. But the long-eared owl (*Asio otus*) takes pride of place. It was in existence at least 36 million years ago in the Oligocene period and it is one of the most ancient of present-day bird species. By Pleistocene times, three million to ten thousand years ago, it is known from fossil discoveries that at least 30 of the present 135 or so owl species were in existence, although the true proportion is likely to be very much higher than this.

Figure 2 is an attempt to portray what is known about the evolution of the owls in relation to some other developments in the living world. Of particular interest is the relative appearance in time of various groups of plants and animals. Flowering plants and trees started to become widespread around 100 million years ago during the Cretaceous period. This was followed some 65 million years ago by the appearance of the rodents which of course feed entirely upon the seeds, leaves and other parts of flowering plants. Interestingly, the owls are thought to have originated at about the same time as the rodents. Most present-day European owl species rely heavily upon voles and to a lesser extent upon rats and mice as a source of food but these particular groups of rodent came into existence well after the origin of the owls. Consequently the first owls must have had a somewhat different diet; perhaps they ate the primitive rodents and also the small insectivorous mammals that existed alongside them.

In addition to the owls two other orders of birds are represented in Figure 2, the nightjars (Caprimulgiformes) and the group which includes falcons, hawks, eagles and vultures (the Falconiformes). These two groups include the nearest living relatives of the owls. In fact at one time some authorities felt that all the birds of prey should be placed within one order. This may seem logical but it is possible that owls and falcons could have had separate ancestors and yet developed similar features such as hooked bills and needle-sharp talons quite independently during the long course of evolution. Such adaptations are necessary requirements, the best and really the only suitable tools for a bird of prey, so why should they not have evolved twice?

Recently a technique has been developed which sheds some light upon the degree of relationship between different groups of birds. It involves chemical analysis of the proteins in the egg white or albumen. These proteins are useful for this type of study because during evolution they probably undergo minor structural alter-ations at a fairly constant rate. As a result, the degree of similarity between the albumen proteins of two species is probably a good indication of the extent of their relationship. Two types of bird with very similar egg albumen proteins are likely to be closely related whilst a third species in which these chemicals show greater structural differences is likely to be a more distant relative. The results of egg albumen protein analysis have revealed several interesting points. Firstly, the owls themselves appear to be a distinctly unified group with no close relatives among other orders of birds. Surprisingly their nearest relatives are not the Fal-coniformes but the Caprimulgiformes (nightjars), a group of insectivorous birds which feed upon the wing, generally being most active at dawn and dusk. The closest link between the owls and the diurnal birds of prey is between the barn owls and the true falcons (the family Falconidae); a number of minor anatomical similarities support this suggested link.

It has been indirectly suggested above that populations of owls, or any type of living organism for that matter, do not stay unchanged over long periods of time. Species are not finite and immutable but liable to change, although this is so slow as to be virtually imperceptible when measured against the human lifespan. Fossils of known and very great age show us that different species existed upon the earth at different times in the distant past and that species do change and have changed over long periods of time. How these changes come about is quite another matter and worthy of mention in the present context.

In the middle of the nineteenth century two outstanding naturalists of the time, Charles Darwin and Alfred Russel Wallace, put forward independently the same suggestion as to how evolution could take place. This suggestion or hypothesis is called natural selection. In essence it is a very simple concept based upon three straight-forward observations and two deductions which can be stated as follows.

Observation 1: all species have a potentially very high reproduc-tive rate. In other words individuals have the capacity to produce very many offspring and they usually do so.

Observation 2: populations of plants and animals may fluctuate but in the long term they stay constant in a stable environment.

Deduction 1: there must be a high rate of mortality among young organisms before they reach an age at which they can start to reproduce.

Observation 3: within a population individuals show variation in observable characteristics and much of this variation is inherited.

Deduction 2: some variants must be better suited to their environment than others and hence stand a better chance of surviving to maturity.

The logical extension of this final point is that when an individual appears which has some new, advantageous feature which is heritable, then the feature concerned is likely to be passed on to future generations and in this way spread through the population.

By way of example, consider a nestling brood of tawny owls. It is possible that there may be some variation in their eyesight. One individual may have poor eyesight compared with the average owl and another may have exceptionally good vision in dim light. At this stage in their lives such variation would probably make very little or no difference to their chances of survival since all their food is brought to them by their parents; they do not have to hunt and so have no need for keen eyesight. But not very long after they have fledged the situation changes, for they have to become independent as summer and autumn pass and learn to catch their own prey. On average a pair of owls will, from a lifetime of nesting attempts, leave behind only two offspring which survive to maturity. So of this brood perhaps only one will be able to find, exploit and defend a suitable territory and survive the rigours of its first winter. The rest are more than likely to perish. Which bird is most likely to survive? Surely the one with the keenest eyesight must have some advantage over its brothers and sisters. If so, and if its acute vision is a heritable characteristic, then it will in the course of time pass on this advantage to its own offspring and in consequence perhaps more than two of these will survive to maturity. In this way any new, advantageous, heritable features which arise in a species will tend to spread through the population over successive generations.

The phrase most frequently applied to the above idea is 'survival of the fittest', meaning an increased chance of survival for those individuals best fitted (i.e. best suited or adapted) to their environment. Survival of the fittest – the biggest and strongest

Short-eared owlets showing effects of asynchronous incubation

individuals, perhaps with the most stamina – may well also take place in the natural world at the expense of the small, weak or sickly, but this is a rather different concept. In this general context owls are particularly interesting because their reproductive strategy is such that these two phenomena may sometimes be in conflict. In most owl species incubation of a clutch starts as soon as the first egg has been laid. This means that hatching takes place over a period of days and consequently the nestlings are not all the same size at any one time. In years when food is anything other than plentiful, the first chick to hatch stands by far the best chance of surviving because, being the biggest, it will take food from the parents at the expense of the other chicks. But being the first to hatch, the biggest and the strongest, has nothing to do with how well fitted to its environment that individual may be during later life. So it would seem that to have a good chance of survival an owlet needs to be the first, or one of the first, in its brood to hatch and it needs to be without any handicaps or disadvantageous features such as poor sight or hearing, even if it has no specifically advantageous characteristics. In addition it needs the ability and possibly the luck to find and hold on to a suitable territory.

To return to the general concept of evolution, that species are liable to change over long periods of time, the implication is that ultimately one species could change into another or possibly one species could be the ancestor of two or even more new ones. The latter could happen if a number of individuals belonging to a species became isolated in some way, for example by colonizing an island. This island population might then follow a separate and quite different evolutionary pathway from that of the mainland species from which it originated. Eventually the result might be a new species quite distinct from the original. The accepted definition of a species is a population of living organisms in which all individuals are potentially capable of interbreeding to produce fully fertile offspring. But in the situations described above there would be continous lines of descent between what we might on this definition recognize as two or more separate species. In this sense the whole idea of species is artificial and a product of the human viewpoint of nature. We perceive evolving life around us as if frozen at a point in time. We see populations as species reproductively isolated from one another rather than as branching lineages stretching through immense, unimaginable periods of time. Yet paradoxically the different types of living organism we recognize and the 'gaps' between them are obviously quite genuine. Moreover, they are real not only to us but also to the organisms themselves.

At this point a problem arises. We know that species change during evolution and yet we classify them on a hierarchical basis from kingdom to species as if they were each quite separate entities that could be slotted into convenient pigeon holes without any difficulty. This situation arose because the present system of classification was initiated before the concept of evolution existed or perhaps when it was just vague imaginings in the minds of a very few men. It was begun by the Swedish naturalist Carolus Linnaeus in 1735, his view of life being that 'there are as many species as the Creator made'. Like other people of his time he regarded species as being finite and immutable, the products of individual and separate acts of creation. With this view of nature his system of classification posed no theoretical problems. Nevertheless, even in the light of present-day knowledge about evolution the system of classification he initiated still serves well enough and it has not been superseded. In all likelihood this is because it is the best attempt that can be made to do the impossible, namely compartmentalize something which is continuous.

2 Characteristics of owls

The ability to fly must have been the subject of countless human dreams. Doubtless this is because in the bird's capacity to soar above the world so many of us see a representation of freedom and perhaps something of that quality which we call life. But for the birds themselves the benefits of flight are more practical. It is of value in escaping from predators and in finding food or even a new place to live, perhaps remote from that in which a bird began its life. However, mastery of the air brings its own limitations for it imposes upon birds severe restrictions in terms of bodily design, and for this reason the anatomy of an owl is much like that of a chaffinch, a duck or any other flying bird. Among the birds there is only one basic body plan. Presumably it is the best and it may even be the only possible design for flight. In contrast, mammals and reptiles show much more diversity of form. Consider a man, a horse and a kangaroo, or a tortoise, a snake and a crocodile.

Owls share with all birds a number of features obviously related to flight such as wings composed of feathers and a very light skeleton, but in fact virtually all parts of the body are adapted for life in the air. The skeleton is modified for both flight and bipedalism (Figure 3), the bones being thin and light. In many cases they are hollow and air-filled with internal struts providing additional support (Figure 4).

The wing is built upon a broadly similar plan to that of the human arm although some bones are fused together and several are absent (Figure 5). There are only three fingers present in a bird's wing, and of these only the second is well developed, the first and third being represented by single bones only. The first digit or thumb is capable of independent movement and with its feathering forms the alula. During flight this structure maintains a smooth flow of air over the wing surface and so helps to prevent stalling. The main wing feathering is borne by the humerus, ulna and hand, the first of these being short and broad to provide a large surface

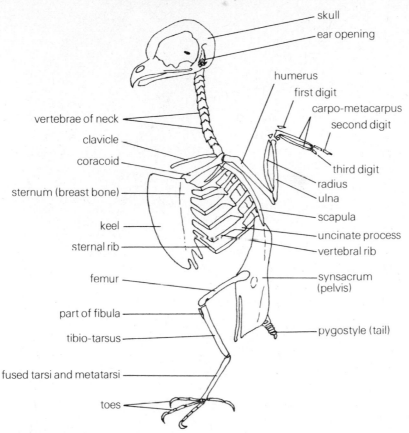

skull
ear opening
humerus
first digit
carpo-metacarpus
second digit
vertebrae of neck
clavicle
coracoid
third digit
radius
sternum (breast bone)
ulna
scapula
keel
uncinate process
sternal rib
vertebral rib
femur
synsacrum (pelvis)
part of fibula
tibio-tarsus
pygostyle (tail)
fused tarsi and metatarsi
toes

Fig 3. Skeleton of an owl

area for the attachment of the flight or pectoral muscles. These of course lie outside the wing itself, in the chest. Other muscles used to alter the position and shape of the wing lie at its base with long tendons running out close to the bones.

Of key importance in flight is the large keeled sternum or breast bone which is the site of anchorage for the flight muscles. In the same plane as the latter are the strut-like coracoid bones. Running from the base of the wing to the sternum these are thick and strong in order to resist compression during flight. There is much fusion of the vertebrae, ribs, shoulder and hip girdles, resulting in a rigid, box-like structure surrounding the internal organs. This structure also serves to resist compression and provides a means by which

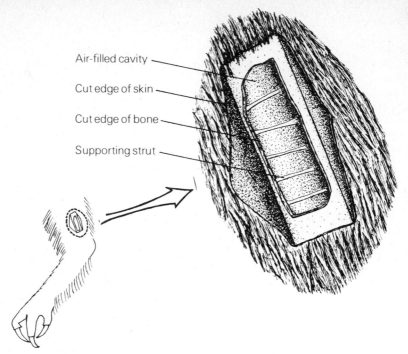

Air-filled cavity

Cut edge of skin

Cut edge of bone

Supporting strut

Fig 4. Internal structure of the tibio-tarsus of tawny owl

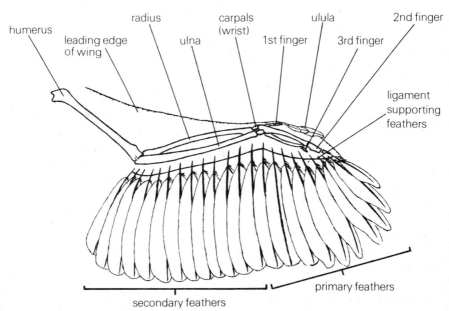

humerus

leading edge
of wing

radius

ulna

carpals
(wrist)

1st finger

ulula

3rd finger

2nd finger

ligament
supporting
feathers

primary feathers

secondary feathers

Fig 5. Flight feathers and skeleton of left wing of tawny owl viewed from below.

thrust from the wings can be transmitted to the rest of the body. Fewer joints also allow simpler musculature and consequently further economy in weight. The ribs are large and have double heads. These form robust joints with the thoracic vertebrae, all but one of which are fused together. From each rib a strut called an uncinate process extends backwards to form a joint with the rib behind. In birds the sternal ribs are bony, unlike those of mammals which are composed of cartilage, and they are jointed to both the vertebral ribs and to the sternum.

Towards the hind end of the body lies the synsacrum. This is a thin, plate-like structure composed of the pelvic girdle fused to 13 of the vertebrae. In the transverse plane the synsacrum is broadly U-shaped, being open below. It surrounds and protects the viscera. The point of anchorage for the tail feathers and musculature, called the pygostyle, is composed of four fused vertebrae. It has to be mobile to allow the tail to steer during flight and it is connected to the synsacrum via six unfused caudal vertebrae.

Of all the backbone, only the neck is long and mobile, allowing freedom of movement of the head. The skull is very thin-walled and light, being strengthened by fusion of the bones from which it is composed. Its functions are to protect the brain, eyes and ears and to support the bill. In owls the eyes are well to the front of the head, allowing a wide field of binocular vision and the skull is relatively short and broad compared with that of most other birds. The absence of teeth also helps to keep weight to a minimum.

Relative to its body weight, the brain of a bird is large, being comparable in size to that of a mammal. A large brain makes possible sophisticated behaviour such as navigation and migration. The cerebellum, which controls movement and balance, is particularly well developed in birds. It is at the back of the brain and is of crucial importance in controlling flight movements. It is likely that a complex and efficient brain was only able to evolve because birds possess a high and constant body temperature. In most birds this is around 42°C, about 5°C higher than that of man. This high body temperature is probably also needed for the pectoral muscles, and to maintain it, highly efficient circulatory and respiratory systems are necessary.

Like mammals, birds possess a four-chambered heart, all blood passing through the lungs to be reoxygenated before it circulates

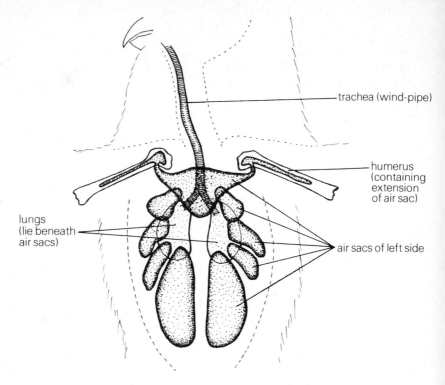

trachea (wind-pipe)

humerus (containing extension of air sac)

lungs (lie beneath air sacs)

air sacs of left side

Fig 6. Air sacs and lungs of an owl

around the rest of the body. The arteries leading to the pectoral muscles are especially large in birds and blood passes along them at high pressure and therefore very rapidly. The normal heart beat rate for a medium sized owl at rest is probably around 300 beats per minute, about four times that of man. This circulatory system supplies not just warmth to the brain, pectoral muscles and other organs but also oxygen and the products of digestion.

The system of air sacs possessed by birds is of key importance in the supply of large quantities of oxygen to the body (Figure 6). Upon inspiration air passes through the lungs and into the air sacs. During expiration it returns, with the result that all inhaled air is removed from the lungs. Compared with mammals very little residual air remains after expiration. It is possible that the air sacs are also involved in temperature control. Excess heat produced during flight may pass out of the body via these structures.

Birds require large quantities of food to maintain their high body temperature and rapid metabolism. Three independent studies have indicated that a barn owl requires about 70 to 100 grammes of food per day, this being 20 per cent or more of the bird's own body weight. This means that digestion has to be very rapid and the barn owl takes less than six hours to process a meal. Indigestible material such as fur, feather and bone remains within the gizzard and is compacted to form a pellet which is subsequently regurgitated. This method of elimination is necessary in owls because they generally swallow their prey whole and large pieces of hard indigestible material such as bone will not pass through the intestines. Contrary to popular belief pellet formation is not unique to birds of prey and over 300 species of bird are known to egest material in this way.

Even the excretory and reproductive systems of birds show weight-saving modifications which assist flight. The urine produced by birds is semi-solid and they do not possess a urinary bladder. In female birds, only one ovary and oviduct are large and functional whilst in males the testes are much reduced in size and dormant outside the breeding season.

The chief distinguishing feature of birds is of course the possession of feathers and in owls these show some interesting specializations. The skin of birds is dry and very thin and from it the feathers grow in much the same way as scales are produced by the skin of a reptile. Moreover these two body coverings are composed of the same chemical, namely keratin, a tough and waterproof protein. Since it is generally accepted that birds evolved from reptiles, then feathers can be regarded as highly modified reptilian scales. It is probable that in the first bird-like creatures the function of the plumage was to prevent heat loss. Only later did the feathers of the hand and arm become enlarged to form a wing.

In most owls the wings are short and broad, their surface area being large for the weight of the bird. This latter feature is described as a low wing-loading. In a barn owl the wing-loading is three kg/m^2, whereas for example that of a duck is about ten kg/m^2. A low wing-loading permits owls to fly in a buoyant fashion with a considerable degree of manoeuvrability, something of particular importance in forest and woodland species. In addition a low wing-loading means that vigorous and rapid beating of the wings

Tawny owl primary feather; the fur-like surface, free barbs on leading edge and frayed trailing edge all contribute to near silent flight

is not necessary. This helps owls to fly quietly which is of great value during nocturnal hunting. It prevents disturbance of prey and interference with the bird's own hearing. To this end the plumage of owls has a number of adaptations. The body feathering is deep and soft, many of the feathers having a fur-like covering on their outer surface. On the leading edge of the primary wing feathers the ends of the barbs do not interlock and form a soft fringe. Similarly the tips of the barbs on the rear or trailing edge are free, resulting in a narrow, fur-like margin. Unfortunately for owls, these sound-deadening adaptations cause more drag or resistance to the air during flight.

Perhaps the two most striking plumage features of owls are the facial discs and ear tufts. Not all species possess the latter, and of Britain's owls only the long-eared and short-eared owls have them. In the long-eared owl each tuft is composed of six narrow feathers. These structures are not ears and they have no association with hearing but appear to fulfil a role in communication. Long-eared owls frequently roost in groups and when relaxed the birds fluff out their plumage and the ear tufts are lowered to a near horizontal position along the top of the head. When an intruder is detected they remain quite still, the plumage is flattened against the body and the ear tufts are raised, perhaps as a warning to other members of the group.

The facial discs are thought to be involved in hearing, probably serving to direct sound into the ear openings (Figure 7). The ruff of feathers around the margin of the disc could be of particular significance in this role. In a resting long-eared owl the radially arranged feathering of the facial disc is somewhat raised causing it to be partially closed, but when the bird becomes alert the facial disc is opened by the feathers being laid flat against the head.

The hearing of owls is particularly acute, especially in some of the more nocturnal species. This adaptation is linked to hunting since small mammals may well be hidden from view beneath grass or other vegetation. The auditory centre in the brain of a barn owl

slit-like ear
opening

shallow
post-aural flap

passage to
ear drum

large forwardly
directed
pre-aural flap

Fig 7. Head of tawny owl with feathering displaced to show ear opening

weighing about 300 grammes contains some 95,000 nerve cells. In
comparison the same area in the brain of a 600-gramme crow is
composed of only about 27,000 cells. Within certain frequencies
the hearing of owls is ten times more sensitive than that of man but
mere registering of sounds is only part of an owl's requirements.
These birds need to pinpoint the source of sounds made by prey
animals with speed and a very high degree of precision.

In most birds the external ear openings are in the form of small
round holes, but in many owl species including the long-eared and
Tengmalm's owls they are crescent shaped slits almost equal to the
height of the skull. They extend from the top of the skull, round
behind the eyes to points level with the lower jaw (Figure 7). In
front of and behind each ear opening there are fleshy flaps called
opercula which are edged with stiff feathers. Changes in the shape
of the facial disc, especially the ruff forming its margin, result from
alterations in the position of these flaps. It is thought that when the
operculum at the front of the ear slit is raised it assists an owl to
pinpoint sounds originating behind its head. A similar effect can be
gained by placing a cupped hand in front of one's ear.

The significance of vertical, slit-like ear openings may be that
they allow a high degree of accuracy in locating prey animals in the
vertical plane. Since owls tend initially to locate and approach prey
such as small mammals at a low angle to the ground, this is of
particular importance. Even a small degree of vertical error would
mean that the owl would swoop down some way in front of or
behind its quarry. On the other hand a similar angle of error in the

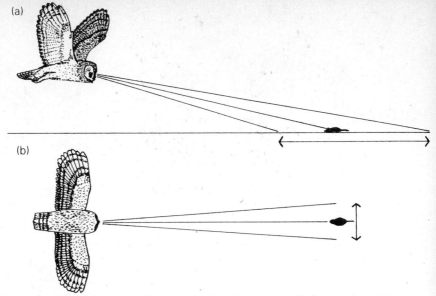

Fig 8. Sound location of prey during hunting: (a) a small degree of vertical error would result in the owl swooping down some way in front of or behind its prey;.(b) a similar horizontal error would result in a lesser degree of inaccuracy along the ground

horizontal plane would result in a lesser degree of inaccuracy along the ground (Figure 8). Furthermore, horizontal error can be more easily corrected during flight than can vertical error.

A further peculiarity of the ears of owls is that in many species they exhibit a degree of asymmetry. In the tawny owl and Tengmalm's owl for example, the cavities leading through the skull to the ear drum are asymmetrical whilst in the long-eared and short-eared owls the external ear openings are asymmetrically positioned (Figure 9). Among the species which exhibit this feature the right ear opening is higher upon the skull than the left by about 10° to 15°, and it is often larger. This asymmetry increases the distance between the ears which means that for any particular sound the difference between what is actually heard by each of them is correspondingly greater. This is of value since the source of a sound is pinpointed by comparing the input received by the two ears and a greater difference between what is heard by the two ears allows increased accuracy in locating the source. Furthermore, asymmetry of the ears means that a moving sound source will result in a rapid decrease in reception in one ear with a smaller decrease or an increase in the other ear. In this way asymmetrical ears amplify differences arising from incorrect orientation of the

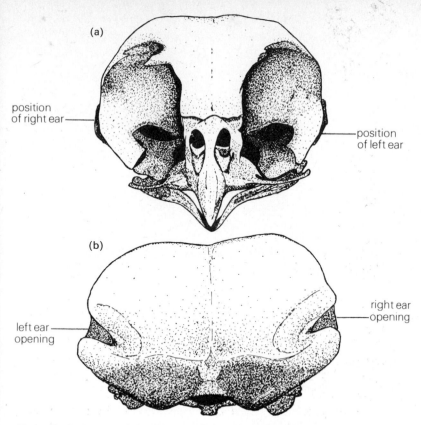

(a)

position
of right ear—

—position
of left ear

(b)

left ear—
opening

right ear
—opening

Fig 9. Skull of tawny owl: (a) viewed from front, (b) viewed from rear, showing the asymmetry of the ear openings. Note that the right side of the skull is slightly larger than the left side

head towards a sound. This assists correct alignment of the head and hence pinpointing of the source.

The range of human hearing extends from approximately 20 to about 15,000 to 20,000 hertz (vibrations per second). In at least some species of owl the auditory spectrum is similar. In the barn owl 20,000 hertz is the upper limit of hearing and captive long-eared owls have been trained to respond to sounds of 18,000 hertz. The lowest pitch audible to the long-eared owl and also to the tawny owl is about 100 hertz which means that these birds cannot hear the lowest notes audible to man, for example the lowest notes of a piano (the range covered by a piano keyboard is 27 to 4,000 hertz). Within the range 2,000 to 6,000 hertz the hearing of tawny and long-eared owls is at its most sensitive and is ten times more acute than that of man. However, human hearing is most sensitive

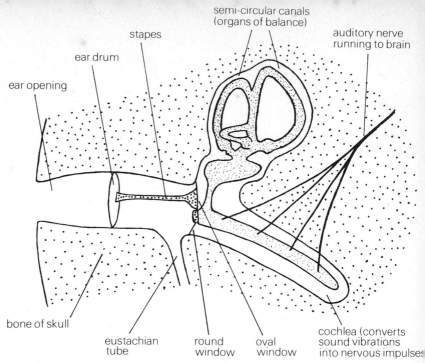

semi-circular canals
(organs of balance)

stapes

ear drum

ear opening

auditory nerve
running to brain

bone of skull

eustachian
tube

round
window

oval
window

cochlea (converts
sound vibrations
into nervous impulses)

Fig 10. Section through the ear of a bird (diagrammatic). Unlike the human ear
the cochlea is not spirally coiled and there is just one bone, the stapes or
columella, in the middle ear, not three

at around 1,000 hertz. The exceptionally keen hearing of owls is
achieved in part by a very complex stapes. This single bone is the
functional equivalent of the three ossicles located in the middle ear
of man (Figure 10). It serves to amplify sound vibrations reaching
the ear drum as it transmits them to the inner ear. In owls,
amplification is by a factor of 65 which is triple that occurring in
the human ear and close to the maximum for optimal transfer of
pressure to the inner ear.

In the barn owl it has been found that at 5,000 hertz each ear has
a wide angle over which hearing is at a maximum sensitivity.
Interestingly, as the pitch rises the angle of maximum sensitivity
becomes progressively narrower, remaining greatest directly in
front of the head. This effect may be a consequence of the slit-like
nature of the ear openings and no doubt it assists in the pinpointing
of high pitched squeaking sounds. Barn owls are capable of
hunting in complete darkness and further experiments have shown
that the ability of these birds to pinpoint sounds is better at higher
frequencies. In one study, captive owls were played recordings of

leaf rustling noises which cut out as soon as the bird left its perch to investigate. Accuracy in locating the source was normally to within an angle of one degree. Consequently the source of the sound must have been located before take off. This fact alone is a clear illustration of the remarkable hearing of owls. If sounds above 8,500 hertz were filtered out from the recordings, locating accuracy was reduced to within only about six degrees. Finally if sounds above 5,000 hertz were filtered out then the birds did not leave their perches at all.

The above study provided further evidence for the reliance owls place upon comparing the input received by each ear. In both owls and man, when the source of a sound is to one side of the head, that sound reaches the closer of the two ears momentarily sooner than the more distant ear. The time difference is about 30 microseconds (i.e. 0.000,03 seconds). Also the ear on the opposite side of the head to the sound source is within a sound shadow. Consequently its perception of the sound is less distinct. However this effect is only marked if the sound waves are smaller than the width of the head. If they are larger then the waves tend to reform behind the head. With reference to the study described above, sounds of around 5,000 hertz have a wavelength of 45 mm which is about the width of the skull of a barn owl. Lower pitched sounds have a longer wavelength and it is probably difficult for owls to locate their source.

A final point of interest relating to the hearing of owls concerns their ability to locate small birds uttering the 'seet' alarm call. This call is made as a warning to others when a predator is in the vicinity. Pinpointing the source of this thin, high pitched note is very difficult for man but it seems unlikely that the same is true for owls in view of their acute hearing. This has been investigated in experiments where a variety of sound recordings were played to captive barn owls and their responses studied. Turning of the head and its correct orientation towards the source of the sound was least frequent for 'seet' and other alarm calls of small birds. Thus the owls could and did locate these calls upon some occasions yet they often made little or no response. An explanation of this paradox is that a barn owl is not likely to capture a small bird that is already alerted. As a result the owl simply takes little notice when it hears an alarm call. If this suggestion is true then it would be of interest to know whether this behaviour pattern is innate or learnt as a result of past hunting experience.

The fact that owls can fly and hunt by night suggests that in addition to acute hearing they must have exceptionally keen eyesight. Their nocturnal habits have no doubt contributed to much of the superstition which surrounds them and also to not a few misconceptions. Owls can see well in dim light and to them a moonlit night probably seems only a little darker than bright sunshine, such is the ability of their eyes to adjust to varying light intensity. However owls cannot see in total darkness any more than man or other animals. Even on moonless nights absolute darkness does not occur, illumination being rarely less than about 37,000 lux. Under carefully controlled experimental conditions it has been demonstrated that both tawny and long-eared owls are able to see under conditions of less than seven lux illumination. This is close to total darkness and quite indistinguishable from it by man. The vision of owls is not hampered by daylight as is commonly supposed and they can see just as well by day as by night. If necessary, nocturnal species are able to hunt successfully by day, for example during summer when the nights are short and they need to supply food for a family. To protect the eyes by day the nictitating membrane or third eyelid can be closed. In owls this structure is opaque. This contrasts with all other birds in which it is transparent. In addition it may be that pigment moves into the retina during daylight hours to protect it from excess light. Another misconception about the eyesight of owls is that they can see infra-red light, something which would be a great asset to any nocturnal animal, but there appears to be no truth in this.

The eyes of owls are very similar to those of man in their basic design (Figure 11). Like the eyes of all birds the front part including the lens and cornea extends forwards so that the eye is not spherical. This shape is maintained by a ring of bones unique to birds and known as sclerotic plates or scleral ossicles. In owls the eyes are in the shape of short, tapered cylinders and the sclerotic plates form a long bony tube. This shape and their large size means that the eyes are rigidly fixed in their sockets and they cannot be turned at all. In compensation the neck is very mobile and the head can be turned through 270° in some species.

Another peculiarity of the avian eye possessed by owls is the

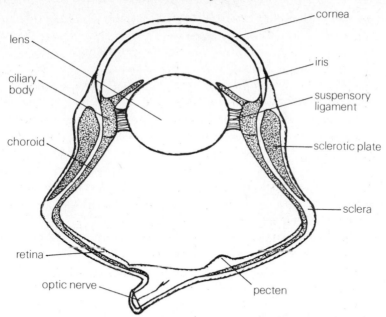

lens

cornea

ciliary
body

iris

suspensory
ligament

choroid

sclerotic plate

sclera

retina

optic nerve

pecten

Fig 11. Horizontal section of right eye of an owl viewed from above

pecten, a structure located upon the retina, close to the optic tract.
It is rich in blood vessels and probably serves to supply the eye
with food and oxygen. In some birds, including diurnal birds of
prey but not owls, it is large and its shape is quite elaborate. In such
cases the pecten is thought to aid the pinpointing of small and
distant moving objects in addition to having a nutritive function.

Among birds, owls have the unusual feature of a wide field of
binocular vision. With the eyes well to the front of the head the
total field of view is 110°, with a binocular field of 70° (Figure 12).
The bill has a steep downward curve which keeps it out of the
visual field. In man the slightly different images perceived by the
two eyes are integrated within the visual centre of the brain to
produce a single image. This greatly improves the appreciation of
depth and distance and is called stereoscopic vision. It seems likely
that the same must be true for owls and other birds of prey but this
is still a poorly understood aspect of vision in birds.

More is known about the way in which the eyes of owls are
adapted to function in dim light. Rods are the principal cell type
present in the retina of owls and are sensitive to variation in light

intensity. The other cell type present, called cones, are associated with colour vision. In man each rod cell is connected to the brain via a separate nerve cell but in owls large groups of rod cells are linked to single nerve cells. This arrangement increases the sensitivity of the eye in dim light. So too does the fact that the retina is relatively close to the lens, making the image which falls upon it small but bright. However, both these features reduce the resolving power of the eye, that is the ability to see fine detail. In compensation the eyes of owls are very large, like those of nocturnal mammals. This helps because the cells making up the retina are a fairly constant size throughout all vertebrate animals so a larger eye has more retinal cells and consequently a greater resolving power.

But how much more sensitive is the vision of owls than that of man? Studies with captive barn owls have helped to provide an answer to this question. During flight these birds can evidently see

Fig 12. Field of view of (a) man (b) owl (c) pigeon
M – area of monocular vision
B – area of binocular vision
X – area not in field of vision

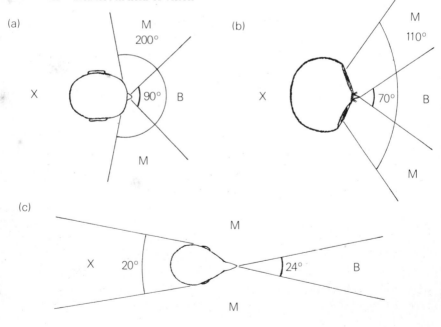

and avoid obstacles with a surface brilliance of 3×10^{-12} lamberts. In comparison the lowest surface brilliance detectable by human eyes is about 1.5×10^{-10} lamberts. Consequently, the barn owl probably has vision 100 times more sensitive than that of man.

Owls, like other birds, are able to see colour. It has been found that the eyes of tawny owls are most sensitive to light in the yellow and yellow-green ranges (around wavelengths 580 nm and 525 nm). Man's maximum sensitivity is to green light (497 nm).

Apart from structural specializations such as sound deadening features of the plumage, exceptional hearing and sight, owls have some unusual adaptations associated with reproduction. Like many birds they hold territories, a feature of obvious value because it allows exclusive hunting over the area held. Furthermore, many owl species nest in tree cavities. Since these are generally few in number it makes sense for an owl to retain throughout the year a territory containing at least one such potential nesting site. Many owls, especially the more nocturnal species, are highly vocal. Hooting and other calls are no doubt associated with the attraction of a mate and also with defence of the territory. The relative importance of these two factors with respect to particular call notes of owls does not seem to be very well understood.

The eggs of owls are white and in most species nearly spherical. Notable exceptions to the latter feature are the eggs of the barn owl and great grey owl which are of a more oval shape. The reasons for these features are not particularly obvious but being white may make it easier for the incubating bird to see the eggs in a dark tree cavity. Most owl species have plumage of a mottled brown colour which makes them well camouflaged when they rest by day but this cryptic colouring is doubly important for species such as the short-eared owl which nests upon open ground.

In many species of owl incubation begins as soon as the first egg has been laid. Since there is a two-day interval or more between the laying of successive eggs this can result in up to three weeks difference in the age of nestlings in large broods. This incubation strategy means that the older and larger chicks will take most of the food supplied by the parents, a fact which is significant in years when prey is anything other than abundant. At such times the older nestlings will survive at the expense of the younger ones. In this way, at least some of the young will fledge. If they were all the same age and size and took similar proportions of the food available then it is likely that they would all starve.

In most owl species incubation is carried out by the female while the male hunts to supply her and later the nestlings with food. Only when the young are quite large does the female leave them and join in hunting. In many types of owl the female is a good deal larger than the male. The reasons for this size dimorphism are uncertain but it appears to be connected with reproduction and diet. One suggestion is that since male owls are the more aggressive sex then pair formation ought to be easier if the female has the compensation of being larger. Another possibility is that the larger female is likely to be better suited to the tasks of incubation and protecting the young whilst the smaller male will be more agile in flight and hence a more efficient hunter. The heavier female may be able to capture larger prey than the male and consequently this resource will remain untapped until she joins in hunting when the young are well grown. In support of the last of these suggestions is the fact that size difference between males and females is greatest in species which feed extensively upon small mammals, for example the short-eared owl, and least in species such as the little owl which feed largely upon insects, none of which will be too big for the male to cope with.

Adaptive radiation of owls

What have been described so far are the general characteristics of owls, but there are of course many variations upon this basic pattern. Owls as a whole are divided into two families (the Tytonidae and the Strigidae) upon the basis of minor but consistent differences in structure (Table 2). These differences have little obvious relevance to the lifestyles of the members of the two families. However, many of the structural peculiarities of individual owl species can be related to their way of life or ecological niche. This is because during the course of evolution each species has become suited to a particular lifestyle, a process known as adaptive radiation.

The family Tytonidae contains the barn owls and the similar bay owls. There are eight species of barn owl distributed throughout all continents except Antarctica whilst the two species of bay owl are restricted to South-East Asia. The barn owl of Britain and Europe (*Tyto alba*) is a species which in many ways might be

TABLE 2 CHARACTERISTICS OF THE TYTONIDAE AND STRIGIDAE

Characteristics	Tytonidae	Strigidae
Relative length of skull	Long	Short
Sternum and clavicle (breast bone and wishbone)	Fused together	Not fused together
Tail	Ends in shallow V	End broadly rounded
Toes	Second and third equal in length	Second toe shorter than third
Third toe	Has comb-like edge	No comb-like edge present

considered a typical owl. It is generally nocturnal, feeds largely upon small mammals and possesses most of the bodily features peculiar to owls. Fossil remains of a now extinct giant barn owl have been found in the West Indies. This bird was larger than any living owl and must have been an impressive sight. The largest living barn owl is the 500-mm long masked owl of Australasia.

Among the Strigidae, by far the largest genus is that including the Eurasian scops owl (genus *Otus*) and about 34 other species. These are generally small, nocturnal owls often feeding upon insects and other invertebrates. They possess ear tufts and tend to have somewhat indistinct facial discs. In North America the counterpart of the Eurasian scops owl is the very similar screech owl (*Otus asio*). Many species of this group are tropical in distribution and some live in semi-desert areas, avoiding the intense heat of the day by their nocturnal habits.

Eagle owls, making up the genus *Bubo*, are the world's largest living owls. The female Eurasian eagle owl measures as much as 710 mm in length and can weigh up to 3.5 kg. In North America this group is represented by the great horned owl (*Bubo virginianus*). Eagle owls are formidable birds, frequently taking prey up to the size of rabbits. They are unusual among owls in having a comparatively small auditory centre in the brain and they seem to hunt largely by sight. This is also the case in the partly diurnal and insectivorous little owl. In Australasia the eagle owls are replaced by the boobook owls (genus *Ninox*). These are of a comparable size, and like the Eagle owls they will often take quite large prey. Another group of fairly large owls found in a different part of the world are the spectacled owls (genus *Pulsatrix*). Inhabiting the rain forests of South America they too have a varied diet including some quite large species such as a group of hedgehog-like, spiny rodents called *Echimys*.

The three species of fishing owl belonging to the genus *Scotopelia* are a further group of large but rather different owls. The most widespread is Pel's fishing owl which measures 500 mm in length. It is found throughout central and southern Africa in forested and wooded areas near rivers. These birds take surface swimming fish using a technique very similar to that of the osprey in which the feet are used to pluck the prey from the water. The legs of fishing owls lack feathers for, if present, these would become waterlogged and fouled with mucus from the skin of fish. The soles of the feet are roughened and spiny and the talons needle sharp, features of great assistance in gripping slippery, struggling fish. Interestingly, the legs and feet of ospreys have the same adaptations. Fishing owls have comparatively small facial discs and like the eagle owls probably place more reliance upon sight than hearing when hunting.

One of the largest of all owls is the snowy owl which may be up to 660 mm in length. It has several special features which equip it for a way of life in the open tundra regions of the northern hemisphere. Most obvious is the white plumage which forms excellent camouflage in such snowbound latitudes and is very thick, covering all the body including the legs and feet. In many owl species gaps appear in the down of the chicks as they grow but in nestling snowy owls this does not happen since the down thickens and grows with the body. Young snowy owls can sit and stand upright at a relatively early age and often lie upon their wings in order to avoid direct contact with the cold ground. The deep, booming call of the snowy owl is said to carry over 11 km. No doubt this powerful call is of value in the defence of the very large territories which these birds hold. The snowy owl inhabits latitudes where daylight is continuous during the summer months and so it is obliged to lead a diurnal existence.

A number of owls have reverted to being active by day, notably the hawk and pygmy owls. The sound deadening plumage adaptations found in most owls are poorly developed or lacking in these species so they are unable to fly silently. Presumably these adaptations are not required by diurnal species which are unlikely to place a great deal of reliance upon their sense of hearing when hunting. The hawk owl is well named since it is in many ways reminiscent of a small hawk, the plumage being compact and strongly barred. In addition it has a long tail, pointed wings and facial discs that are poorly developed. The 12 species of pygmy owl (genus *Glaucidium*) found throughout the world are fearless birds of around 150 mm in length. They have proportionately very large, powerful feet and will sometimes prey upon mammals weighing almost as much as themselves. The world's smallest owl, the least pygmy owl (*Glaucidium minutissimum*) is a member of this group. It is just 120 mm in length and inhabits Mexico and the Amazon valley. Elf owls (genus *Micrathene*) of southern U.S.A. and South America are comparable in size to pygmy owls but are more lightly built and feed chiefly on insects.

On the plains of the Americas there occurs one of the most unusual of all owl species, the burrowing owl (*Speotyto cunicularia*). As its name suggests, this owl nests in burrows. It sometimes constructs these itself using its very long and powerful legs, but more often it takes over or shares those of the marmot. Burrowing owls can of course flee from danger by taking to the air but often use their long legs to run quickly to the safety of a burrow.

Finally some mention must be made of the remaining groups of owls which have representatives in Europe. These are the *Strix* owls, the eared owls (genus *Asio*) and Tengmalm's owl. The *Strix* owls include the tawny, great grey and Ural owls. All eleven members of this genus lack ear tufts and all have dark eyes except the great grey owl which has yellow eyes. The reason for this exception is obscure. Many of these birds are widespread in distribution and have diets which vary a good deal with location and habitat. The great grey owl is something of an exception since it preys very largely upon voles in spite of its apparently large size. Beneath its thick plumage however this owl is a slim and lightly built bird and although equal in length to the eagle owl it weighs only about half as much. Its long fine talons are well suited to a diet of small mammals and contrast markedly with those of the eagle owl which are much thicker and more robust. The tawny owl is the only member of this group with a range which extends into North Africa. Further south it is replaced by the wood owl (*Ciccaba woodfordii*), a bird which also inhabits South America. In North America the barred owl (*Strix varia*) is said to be the most common owl species east of the Rocky Mountains. Its diet is varied, it is normally nocturnal and usually nests in a tree cavity.

The two species of eared owl (genus *Asio*) found in Britain and Europe show some interesting contrasts. The short-eared owl is a bird of grassland whilst the long-eared owl is a forest dweller. The former has longer, narrower wings which suit it to its open habitat and nomadic, migratory existence, whereas the long-eared owl is sedentary and its shorter, broader wings equip it for manoeuvrability when flying among trees.

The smallish Tengmalm's owl of Europe belongs to the genus *Aegolius*. In many ways similar to the tawny owl it also occurs in North America where it is known as the boreal owl. Here its smaller relative, the saw-whet owl is also to be found. Two other, very similar members of this group inhabit parts of Central and South America.

Thus it can be seen that a good deal of variation exists among the world's 135 or so species of owl. It is difficult to provide an exact figure for the number of living owl species, partly because it is not entirely certain whether some forms should be ranked as races or distinct species. Also a few species of owl are extremely rare and sadly they are threatened with the possibility of extinction. On the other hand it is quite likely that there are some types of owl in the remoter parts of the world which have yet to be discovered by man. Within recent years two such finds have been made, both in the cloud forests of Peru. The first was a tiny owl named *Xenoglaux loweryi* which is similar to the elf owls, and the second was a new species of screech owl (*Otus marshalli*). First descriptions of these birds were published in 1977 and 1981 respectively. Much more could be written about the diversity of owls, especially concerning nesting habits and detailed differences in diet. These features characterize what might be called the lifestyle of a bird, or more properly its ecological niche. This aspect, the ecology of British and European owl species, forms the subject of a later section.

3 Owls resident in Britain

BARN OWL (*Tyto alba*)

The common name of this owl refers to one of its favourite roosting and nesting places, for indeed the barn owl seems to prefer man-made habitations to natural ones for these purposes. It is also known as the white owl and the screech owl, these being descriptions of its general appearance and call. The scientific name for the barn owl is *Tyto alba* which means white owl; *Tyto* from the Greek *tuto*, a kind of owl, and *alba* from the Latin *albus* meaning white. This may be the species which gave rise to the superstitious belief that owls are omens of death and ill fortune. Its ghostly features are obvious: silent flight, pale colour, a call note which is a long drawn out shriek and its tendency to inhabit derelict or little used buildings and sometimes church towers. There are even reports of luminous barn owls which, bizarre though they may seem, are likely to be genuine; the effect may result from luminous bacteria, present in the decaying wood of hollow roosting trees, becoming rubbed on to the feathers.

The upper-parts of the barn owl are orange buff, spotted and marked with grey and white whilst the under-parts are white with just a few dark grey spots. The face is also white with a rust-coloured border and relatively small, black eyes, the bill being white and partly hidden by a row of white feathers on either side. The legs are clad in white hair-like feathers down to the feet which are dark coloured with brown claws. The barn owl is a medium-sized owl, being about 350 mm long. Males, females and fully grown juveniles are all similar in size and appearance, although on average females tend to be slightly larger and have somewhat greyer upper-parts. It is a relatively long-winged owl with a wingspan of around 760 mm. The face is heart shaped and these owls do not have ear tufts. The legs are relatively long and when at rest the feet are placed slightly apart so that from the front the legs sometimes appear to slope towards one another resulting in a 'knock-kneed' appearance. When perching, two toes are posit-

43

ioned in front and two behind but when on a flat surface the toes are spread out fairly evenly. In this species the tail ends in a shallow V, unlike all other European owls in which the tail is rounded.

The barn owl occurs throughout most of the British Isles. In England and Scotland it is relatively less abundant in the east between the Wash and the Humber and from the Tees to the Firth of Forth. It is absent from parts of northern and eastern Scotland and from the Hebrides.

The barn owl is an extremely widespread species. In Europe its range extends as far north as Scotland and southern Sweden to the south-west of the U.S.S.R. Outside Europe it occurs in most of North and South America and in many parts of Africa including Madagascar. It is also found on the Indian subcontinent, in Malaysia and Australasia. Not surprisingly, with this worldwide range there is a good deal of variation in its appearance from one geographical region to another. In all, more than 35 subspecies or races have so far been recognized on the basis of slight but constant differences in external features. The race to be found in Britain and described above is the white breasted barn owl (*Tyto alba alba*, the third name indicating the subspecies). The other principal European subspecies is the dark breasted form, *Tyto alba gutatta* (*gutatta* meaning spotted from the Latin *gutta* for spot, this referring to the bird's thickly spotted under-parts).

The white breasted barn owl occurs in south-west Europe, western France and the British Isles. The dark breasted form is found in the north and east of Europe, namely southern Sweden, Holland, Germany, the Alps, Austria, Poland, western U.S.S.R., Hungary and Bulgaria. Its range overlaps with that of the white breasted form in eastern France, Belgium and West Germany, and in many other parts of Europe both forms are common. It would be of great interest to know to what extent the two forms interbreed in the wild and how the colour patterns are inherited. Since individuals of intermediate colouration do not seem to occur, one of the two colour patterns is presumably dominant to the other in situations of hybridization. Individuals of the dark breasted race have occasionally been seen in southern and eastern England during autumn and winter when these birds are more inclined to wander out of their normal range.

Barn owl with young

The dark breasted form has orange buff under-parts which are thickly covered with dark spots. Its facial disc is also orange buff towards the centre but pales to off-white towards the margin. There is a dark patch between the bill and each eye. The facial ruff is red-brown, the feathers having dark tips. Its upper-parts are greyer than those of the white breasted form, with black spots and whitish tips to the feathers. Adults have a wingspan which is on average slightly larger than that of the white breasted form.

In general the barn owl is a bird of open land compared, for example, with the tawny owl which is very much a woodland species. It inhabits agricultural land, meadows, open parkland, grassland, heaths, semi-deserts and sometimes coastal plains. The barn owl is normally nocturnal but it will remain active and hunt during daylight in exceptionally cold weather if food is hard to find and also when feeding young in summertime when the nights are short and large quantities of prey are required. Typical roosting sites are ruined buildings, barn lofts, church towers, hollow trees and caves or crevices in rocky outcrops. Birds usually roost alone or in pairs but small groups have been recorded occasionally. This may reflect a shortage of suitable sites in the areas concerned rather than a genuine tendency to be gregarious.

Barn owls normally become active just before darkness and they hunt by quartering the ground with a slow, flapping flight alternating with gliding and occasional hovering of a laboured appearance. They rarely rise more than a few metres above the ground when hunting and frequently stop to perch on a post, stump or other vantage point where an upright posture is assumed. Individuals often hunt regularly over a particular area of land and will frequently cover this several times in the course of a night. Barn owls are capable of hunting on moonless nights, when presumably they rely a good deal upon their highly acute hearing. The extent of their general dependence upon the dim light of dawn, dusk and also the moon is not really known. It is possible that their silent appearance and shrieking call may be a combination which makes prey animals too terrified to move. Small mammals which make up most of the diet are caught by the owl dropping swiftly, opening its wings only at the last moment in order to brake as it grasps the prey with its talons. The food is often eaten where it is caught or else carried just a short distance to a more sheltered position. Small birds which are generally a minor item of diet are snatched from their roosting perches in shrubs, and barn owls have been seen to beat their wings against foliage in order to flush out sleeping birds. Presumably these are then caught on the wing as they flee.

The barn owl regurgitates large pellets, about 50 mm long and 25 mm in diameter, which are black and glossy. The reason for this peculiar appearance is unclear. The pellets are usually produced at a rate of two per 24 hours at the roost site, and as individuals tend to roost in the same place regularly over long periods of time, this makes systematic collection of pellets and their analysis relatively easy. Much has been learnt from this type of study and it is evident that although diet in the barn owl varies with local habitat, in general mammals form the large majority of the prey. Species recorded include the common, pygmy and water shrews, the mole, the short-tailed, bank and water voles, the rat, wood mouse, house mouse and harvest mouse. Remains of birds found in pellets include those of the starling, robin, blackbird, pied wagtail, skylark, various thrushes, finches, pipits and warblers. More unusual prey items are bat species, rabbits, fish and frogs. It would be of interest to know to what extent birds and also bats are caught upon the wing. Beetles and moths also form part of its diet.

The swallowing capacity of the barn owl is considerable. T. A. Coward (Coward, 1964) described a captive bird which habitually

Incubating barn owl

swallowed entire rats, leaving just the tail protruding from its bill whilst the rest of the carcass underwent digestion. Finally after a period of several hours the skin and skeleton were regurgitated.

In the British Isles a large scale survey into the diet of the barn owl carried out by D. E. Glue of the British Trust for Ornithology indicated that the short-tailed vole is the most important prey species in most areas. Where these are absent either the brown rat, the common shrew or the wood mouse (which is not exclusively a woodland mammal) usually assumes primary importance. For example in Ireland and the Isle of Man, the short-tailed vole and also the common shrew are absent and the chief prey species are the brown rat and the wood mouse. It seems that on average birds form only about two per cent of the total bulk of prey taken.

The barn owl is generally a silent bird but as noted above its normal note is a long drawn shriek, often uttered in flight. Less frequently it utters a sharp 'kee-yak' and also makes a variety of noises such as bill snapping, hissing and snore-like sounds. To what extent these various calls are associated with courtship and territorial defence seems to be unknown. In Britain breeding begins in April or early May but little is known about the initial courtship. Aerial wing clapping has been recorded in this species and food items left at the breeding site have been noted, suggesting ritual presentation of food to the female by the male. Pairing often lasts for life as is the case with most owls.

Nest sites are similar to those selected for roosting which are described above. Additionally, nest-boxes are quite readily used by this species (designs for nest-boxes are described in the final chapter). No nest as such is built, the eggs being laid on an accumulation of pellets. On rare occasions barn owls have been known to use an old jackdaw's nest. The eggs are elliptical (40 × 32 mm) which is unusual for an owl, those of most species being almost spherical. Normally four to six eggs are laid but there may be as few as three or as many as eleven. Initially they are dull white but gradually they become stained yellow. The eggs are laid at approximately 48 hour intervals, incubation often starting as soon as the first egg has been laid, a feature typical of owls. The male takes no part in incubation other than to bring food to the sitting female. The eggs take about 33 days to hatch and the young are in the nest for anything between nine and twelve weeks, this presumably depending upon the abundance of food and their consequent rate of growth. As incubation begins when the first egg is laid, nestlings hatch at different times and at any one time are of differing sizes. Not surprisingly the larger individuals take most of the food brought to the nest by the parents and consequently stand by far the best chance of surviving to the fledgling stage, especially in years when food is scarce. At such times the smaller individuals may die and can be eaten by the hungry, older nestlings. This may seem harsh from a human viewpoint but it means that the older birds have a better chance of survival. When newly hatched, the young are clad in thick white down but during their first two weeks of life this is gradually replaced by a longer, creamy white down.

Both parents hunt to feed the young and supplying enough prey can become a problem when the nestlings are large and the summer nights short. This is one of the most likely times to see a hunting barn owl on the wing during daylight hours. Attendant adults will usually leave the nest before an intruder becomes too close but on occasions they will display aggressively. When doing so the bird lies down or crouches with the wings spread and sways its head from side to side, hissing and snapping its bill. A second brood is not unusual when food is abundant. In such circumstances the eggs may be laid at any time from June to August. Normally the average fledging rate is about 4.5 individuals per brood, so in a good year each pair may raise nine young to this stage.

Since the beginning of this century there has been concern about the decline of the barn owl in Europe. In 1932 the Royal Society for the Protection of Birds carried out a survey into the status of this species in Britain. This was one of the first studies of its kind. The estimated barn owl population of England and Wales was 25,000 and a general decrease in numbers was apparent, except in

48

1. Barn owl with short-tailed vole (Microtus agrestis)

2. Dark-breasted form of the barn owl (Tyto alba guttata)

3. *Adult male snowy owl*

4. *Pair of snowy owls at their nest; the male is carrying a lemming*

5. Little owl and young at their nest

6. Tawny owl; the very large, dark eyes are a striking feature

7. *Tawny owl and young at nest in tree cavity*

8. *Long-eared owl with well-grown nestlings. The adult's ear tufts are laid flat across the top of its head; the brilliant orange eyes are a distinctive feature of this species*

Northumberland and the north-west of England where these birds appeared to be increasing. A variety of causes were likely to have contributed to the general decrease in population up to that date, including hunting, gamekeeping, taxidermy, collecting and, perhaps more importantly, loss of suitable habitat for these birds. A general but long term decline in numbers of barn owls in Europe as a whole probably reflects the slow but progressive loss of suitable nest sites. In Britain at least, this regrettable trend appears to be accelerating at the present time.

SNOWY OWL (*Nyctea scandiaca*)

The snowy owl is a very large, white owl of the sub-arctic. It retains a tenuous hold upon its status as a British resident; in recent years a few birds have remained throughout the summer on the Shetland Islands and one pair bred on Fetlar from 1967 until 1975. Elsewhere in Britain the snowy owl is a winter rarity.

With a wingspan of around 1.52 metres and a length of 533 to 660 mm, this bird is comparable to the eagle owl in size and is in fact one of the largest owl species in the world. The adult male is a pure, uniform white, sometimes with just a few small brown markings. The female is similarly coloured but with the addition of dark brown barring on the breast, upper-parts and wings. These markings are most prominent in winter, for during the summer months the colour fades and is also lost to some extent by abrasion of the feathers. Both male and female have very small ear tufts which are not easily seen and an unusual feature of this species is the incomplete nature of the facial disc. The feathering above the eyes is normal and not arranged radially as in the rest of the disc. The eyes are bright yellow, the bill and also the claws being dark brown. White colouration is of value to the snowy owl because it helps to camouflage the bird when hunting. The barring of the female renders her better hidden when nesting upon open ground often amid a partial covering of snow. Being white is of further help to these birds since it aids heat conservation; less heat is lost by radiation from a white surface than from any other colour. Also there are air spaces in white feathers which contribute to the insulating power of the plumage. Not surprisingly the legs and feet of the snowy owl are heavily feathered and all of the plumage is very thick and downy. However it does moult in summer.

The snowy owl has a range stretching right around the northern hemisphere and extending south to a latitude of about 60°N in the Shetland Islands, eastern Siberia and Hudson's Bay. In Europe it is to be found as a breeding species principally in Norway. It breeds as far north as Peary and Germania Lands which form part of northernmost Greenland. With such a range the bird is subjected to the perpetual daylight of arctic summers and is of necessity diurnal. Its scientific name is associated with its range, as *Nyctea scandiaca* means Scandinavian night (*Nyctea* from the Greek *nuktios* meaning night, and *scandiaca* from the Latin *Scandia*, the ancient name for the southernmost part of Sweden).

In the British Isles the snowy owl is generally an uncommon winter visitor. Those seen in eastern counties are probably from Eurasia whilst birds reaching Ireland and the west coast of Britain are more likely to originate from Greenland or North America. From 1900 to 1962 there were only six records of snowy owls in Britain, four of these being in the period 1958 to 1962. From 1962 until 1966, 20 records were accepted and then in the summer of 1967 a pair nested on Fetlar and raised five offspring. Nesting took place every year until 1975 and a total of 21 young were reared during this period. Unfortunately the adult male drove off all his younger rivals and when he himself finally disappeared there was no potential mate available for the two adult and three immature females which remained in 1976.

The increase in the number of sightings during the 1960s and the nesting upon Fetlar were probably a response to a period of generally cooler climate, allowing or encouraging these birds to extend their range southwards. This period of nesting was possibly not a unique event in Britain for it is reputed that snowy owls nested on Fetlar in 1859 and 1871. It should be remembered that the Shetlands are only some 300 miles from Hardanger Vidda in Norway, the nearest breeding ground of the snowy owl. This is a small distance for a large bird prone to nomadic movements in winter, so it is quite possible that the snowy owl has nested on the Shetlands in the more distant past and it may well do so again in the future. Palaeolithic cave paintings in Les Trois Frères in Ariège, southern France, depict a pair of snowy owls with their young, an

Last brood of snowy owls to be reared on Fetlar (Shetland Islands) in recent years in July 1975

indication that when the climate of Europe was much colder, the snowy owl's range extended further south than at present.

The territory of the snowy owl is very large and even when food is abundant the maximum density of breeding birds is about one pair per nine to ten km². Not surprisingly, sound communication plays an important part in the defence of such large areas and the male snowy owl has a call which carries long distances across the open land of its tundra breeding grounds. This call is composed of three harsh shrieks followed by a lower note. In addition the male will make a low, hissing grunt and both males and females utter a high pitched laughing call. The snowy owl will call from the ground or from a perch unlike the short-eared owl, its open ground counterpart in temperate regions, which calls in flight.

The snowy owl nests on the ground, generally upon rocky outcrops or other slightly elevated ground which allows a view of the surrounding area. As is usual in owl species the female incubates the eggs while the male hunts to provide her with food. When not hunting he guards the nest site, taking up a position on one of a series of chosen vantage points nearby. Breeding success is linked to food supply, in particular the abundance of lemmings which are one of the chief prey items of the snowy owl. Usually four or five eggs are laid but when lemmings are numerous a clutch of up to nine may be produced. They are laid between April and June and incubation begins as soon as the first egg has been laid, taking about 32 to 34 days per egg.

The young are initially clad in a white down, but this soon turns dark grey except for the feathering of the facial disc, throat, legs and toes which remains white. For the first seven to ten days of life the young are fed with small pieces of meat carefully prepared by the female. Only when they are larger do the parents include bones, fur and feathers in the diet of their offspring. The young disperse from the nest some weeks before they can fly at a time when their first true plumage is beginning to develop. This is similar to that of the adult female, being white, barred with dark brown and it is normally complete by about October. At this early stage of life when it is just beginning to develop, this feathering forms an excellent camouflage as the young crouch amid patches of snow upon rocky ground covered with mosses and lichens.

Young snowy owls are vulnerable to predators and the parents will bark and dive at intruders in an attempt to drive them away. The female will also challenge potential predators upon the ground. She does this by rushing toward them, bill open and head held low with her wings arched upwards over her back. The adults also have a distraction display in which the bird feigns injury in an attempt to lure predators away from the young. When an intruder approaches, the female will make a long whistling call which is a signal for the young to hide. In spite of all this care by the parents, predation of unfledged snowy owls is heavy, their principal enemies being arctic foxes and skuas.

The chief prey of the snowy owl is the lemming of which there are several species within its large, circumpolar distribution. Where lemmings are absent the snowy owl is either rare, as for example in Iceland, or else it is not to be found at all, as is the case on Jan Meyen and Franz Josef Land. Lemming populations fluctuate considerably in size, building up to a peak about every four years before their well known migrations take place. For the snowy owls in the area concerned the autumn following such an emigration is not surprisingly a period of hardship. At such times the owls rely more heavily upon other species such as voles, arctic hares and in North America the snowshoe rabbit.

In winter many snowy owls move southwards but some winter in sub-arctic regions, subsisting upon arctic hare and ptarmigan. The snowy owl will occasionally take fish and there is a record from Iceland of one bird taking a char in the manner of an osprey, snatching the fish from the water and carrying it away in its talons. The diet of the Shetland snowy owls was inevitably different from normal. Here they were noted to have fed upon rabbits, mice and various birds including redshank, lapwing, oystercatcher, rock dove and arctic skua. When small the young were provided with wood mice then later with rabbits and birds. Snowy owls are able to catch birds in flight but take most of their prey from the ground. When hunting they can hover, surprising for such a large bird.

Within their normal range the cyclical crash in numbers of lemmings results in snowy owls tending to wander more extensively and in greater numbers during the winters concerned. Such movements are known as irruptions and their magnitude depends upon the abundance of other food in winters when lemmings are scarce. The arctic hare population falls to a minimum about once every ten years and if this coincides with a crash in lemming numbers then the snowy owl irruption is consequently on a larger scale. It is at such times that snowy owls are more frequently seen outside their normal range. Such large scale irruptions are more extensive in North America, for example over 2,300 sightings were recorded in the U.S.A. during the winter of 1926–7, a country well outside the normal range of the snowy owl. Wintering snowy owls have even been recorded in California and Bermuda. In Europe the most southerly record is for a bird seen in the Azores but the more usual irruptive wintering zone includes Sweden, Norway, Denmark, Finland and Germany with some birds occasionally reaching France and Britain.

LITTLE OWL (*Athene noctua*)

The association between owls and wisdom is an ancient one and it is probable that the little owl was the first species to be involved in this symbolism. Many coins from ancient Athens bear the image of Athene the goddess of wisdom accompanied by a little owl and it is from this deity that the bird received its generic name. In the realm of children's stories this association has been transferred to either an eared owl or else one similar to a tawny.

Two subspecies of this owl occur in Europe, that found in Britain and western Europe being named *Athene noctua vidalii*. *Noctua* is Latin for a type of night owl and Ignatius Vidal was Director of the Zoological Museum of Valencia when this bird was given its name in 1857. The other subspecies is to be found in dry and sandy areas of the eastern Mediterranean region and is much paler than the western form.

The little owl is about the size of a song thrush, being approximately 216 mm long with a wingspan of about 500 mm and weighing 140 grammes. Its upper-parts are dark-brown mottled with white, the pale markings on the head being in the form of streaks whilst the wings and tail are barred white and brown. The under-parts are pale and streaked with brown. The facial disc of the little owl is poorly developed and its upper edge has pale feathering giving the impression of thick, horizontal eyebrows below which are the bright yellow eyes and yellow bill. It appears to have a somewhat flat top to its head and lacks ear tufts. The legs are covered in a pale, hairy down and are relatively long; the little owl is able to run quite fast along the ground when hunting for insects. When perched it adopts an upright posture whereas in flight its rounded wings and very short tail are distinctive features.

In Britain the little owl is common as far north as Yorkshire, although it occurs in lesser numbers as far north as Midlothian in Scotland. This owl is absent from Ireland. Elsewhere it occurs throughout Europe as far north as Denmark, being a vagrant in Sweden where it has bred on occasions. Its range is generally within latitudes 30°N and 55°N. Outside Europe this includes North Africa and a band across Asia to the Pacific coast. Within this large range ten subspecies have been described on the basis of differences in size and colouration. The little owl is generally sedentary although there may be some dispersion outside the breeding season. In Britain its most usual habitat is well wooded farmland although it is occasionally seen in parks and gardens throughout its European range. Outside Europe it is frequently a bird of open habitats such as steppe and semi-desert but it is generally not found at high altitudes nor within forested areas.

Two factors which affect the status of the little owl in Europe are the severity of winter weather and human disturbance. Many birds are killed by harsh winters not only in Britain but in western and central Europe generally. Nevertheless the population as a whole evidently has the capability to recover since it remains stable in the long term. Disturbance is a more serious problem in parts of its range such as some areas of West Germany where it is at present considered to be an endangered species.

The little owl is not a species native to Britain. Various attempts were made to introduce it during the nineteenth century and breeding by released birds took place in Kent in 1879. Introductions successful in the long term took place from 1888 to 1890 in Northamptonshire and during the ensuing ten years in Hampshire, Herefordshire and Yorkshire. The little owl then took about 15 years to establish itself after which came the main period of its expansion between 1910 and 1930. It was introduced into Britain by Lord Lilford and others because of its known value as a predator of mice and insect pests. Indeed, due to its beneficial effects it is encouraged by Dutch farmers and is protected by law in Germany, Hungary and Switzerland. As long ago as 1842 the naturalist Charles Waterton wrote of this bird, 'This diminutive rover of the night is much prized by the gardeners of Italy for its uncommon ability in destroying insects, snails, slugs, reptiles and mice. There is scarcely an out-house in the gardens and vineyards of that country which is not tenanted by the [little owl].'

Nevertheless, great controversy surrounded the introduction of the little owl into Britain, there being accusations of it taking large numbers of game and poultry chicks. It was also blamed for the decline in numbers of some wild bird species. Consequently an investigation into the diet of the little owl was organized by the British Trust for Ornithology, the results being published in 1936 and 1937. The survey involved the analysis of nearly 2,500 pellets, the stomach contents of 28 owls found dead and remains of prey from 76 nest sites. The results indicated that the diet of the little owl consists largely of earwigs and beetles. Only seven pellets contained the bones of poultry chicks and two the remains of young game birds. Hence the little owl was shown to be very largely beneficial in its feeding habits. The diet is in fact about half insects, notably earwigs, beetles (especially cockchafers), craneflies and moths. Slugs, snails and earthworms, which the little owl will hunt on foot, are also eaten, as are voles, mice and young rats. Birds up to those of its own size are taken occasionally, particularly it would seem during the breeding season. Not surprisingly the diet of the little owl varies with habitat. Lizards are eaten where these are plentiful and bat species were first recorded as an item of diet as recently as 1971, in Greece.

The pellets of the little owl are grey and about 30 to 40 mm long

Little owl with earthworm; these can form a significant part of the diet

and 10 to 15 mm in diameter which is comparatively small. They are usually rounded at both ends but sometimes drawn out to a point at one end, much like those of the kestrel.

The little owl is active by day as well as by night but it hunts mainly at dawn and dusk. It does so from a perch by watching for movements on the ground below. By day one can often encounter this bird perched upon some vantage point. When approached it displays little fear and will move its head up and down and from side to side as it scrutinizes the intruder. If one continues to approach it will take off suddenly and fly away in a low and undulating fashion. Being active by day, the little owl is prone to mobbing by small birds.

The call of this owl is a low and plaintive 'kiew-kiew'. There is also an infrequent song similar to the first part of the song of a curlew, but how these are related to territorial defence and courtship is unclear. In Britain the little owl nests up to an altitude of 320 metres and hence it is a bird of lowland areas. Typically the nest is in a hole in a tree but other, similar sites are sometimes used such as wall cavities and even rabbit burrows. Very occasionally it will use the old nest of another species such as the jackdaw or stock dove. A survey of the breeding habits of the little owl in Britain was published in 1980, the results showing that about three-quarters of all nests are in well-wooded farmland. Furthermore 92 per cent of nests, irrespective of habitat type, were in deciduous tree cavities, principally in oak, ash and willow.

The eggs of the little owl are dull white and broadly elliptical, being about 38 mm long. Normally three to six are laid, the maximum recorded being nine. Incubation occasionally begins as soon as the first egg has been laid as is typical of owls, but more often the female does not begin to sit until the clutch is complete. The incubation period is 28 to 33 days per egg. In Britain egg laying may commence at any time from mid March until mid June, however the majority of clutches are started in late April and early May. In more southerly parts of Europe the peak egg laying period is earlier in the year. When the young first hatch they have a white or creamy down but later this becomes a red-grey colour. Young little owls fledge after about 32 to 34 days in the nest, this period varying with clutch size and the abundance of food. They are able to fly strongly by about one week after leaving the nest and normally disperse after about four to five weeks.

Normally a pair of little owls will raise just one brood in a year but two have been recorded and eggs have been laid as late as September in years when food is very abundant, for example during mouse and vole 'plagues'.

The little owl will take to nest-boxes and has indeed shown a distinct preference for these in one study carried out in Friedrichshafen in West Germany. Here, as a result of the provision of suitable nesting 'tubes', the number of birds nesting within the study area increased from four pairs in 1972 to twenty pairs in 1976. During 1975 and 1976 as many as six pairs nested within one km², the distance between nests being as little as 120 metres. Four pairs of birds nested within the study area for a period of three years. Breeding was very successful, the average clutch size being

4.4 eggs, and about two-thirds of the young survived to the fledging stage which represents an average of 2.84 young fledged per brood. The main cause of nestling death was found to be periods of prolonged rain, presumably because this makes it more difficult for the adults to find sufficient food for their offspring.

The use made of nest-boxes in this study suggests that perhaps the availability of suitable tree cavities is the main factor limiting the number of breeding pairs of little owls in many areas. The removal of aged trees as part of a general tidying up of farmland and other habitats would not then be in the interests of this bird. Furthermore, nest-boxes could be of considerable value to the little owl in areas where natural nest sites are few in number.

TAWNY OWL (*Strix aluco*)

In Britain this is perhaps the most familiar of owl species if only because of its soft, musical call, for this is the owl which hoots. Walk through almost any stretch of deciduous woodland in Britain on a mild autumn night and you are quite likely to hear one. The note is perhaps better described as a soft and tremulous 'oo-oo-oo-ooooooo'. Interestingly, the other chief call note of this bird is a sharp 'ke-wick' and it has been suggested that 'tu-whit, tu-whoo' is in fact a combined description, one bird calling and a second answering: 'ke-wick', 'oo-oo-oo-ooooooo'.

The tawny owl is perhaps the most widely used name for this bird but it is also known as the brown owl or wood owl. *Strix aluco*, its scientific name, means screech owl (from the Greek *strizo*, to screech). Again this is a fair description of some of the bird's calls, however the common name screech owl is sometimes applied to the barn owl (*Tyto alba*).

Mottled in warm brown, rufous and buff, the tawny owl gives the appearance of quite a large, thick-set bird with a short rounded tail, large head and relatively short neck. The latter feature is a result of the thick plumage as the neck is in fact quite long and very flexible. The tawny owl is able to turn its head through nearly 180°, compensation for the bird's somewhat restricted angle of vision and its inability to move the eyes within their sockets. In flight the wings of the tawny owl appear short, broad and rounded. It flies with wing-beats that are fairly slow, regular and virtually silent.

The sexes are similar and the overall size range is 355 to 405 mm in length, the female being slightly larger than the male. The female weighs 410 to 800 grammes and the male 410 to 550 grammes. The plumage of the upper-parts is generally dark brown, mottled with a rusty brown. There are noticeable light bars on the wings formed by buff tips to the secondary feathers. The tail is similarly barred. The under-parts are buff, striated and lightly barred with dark brown, the legs and feet being completely feathered. The facial disc is grey-brown with a dark brown margin and the yellowish horn-coloured bill is almost hidden beneath the plumage. Two distinctive features of this species are the relatively very large dark eyes and the absence of ear tufts.

The young are at first clad in white down which later becomes barred with buff. When this is moulted they have a greyish, barred plumage. Some adults retain a greyish colouration but this is unusual in British birds and a relatively more frequent occurrence in the rest of Europe.

The tawny owl is widely distributed and a common bird in most of Britain but it is relatively scarce in the south-west and absent from the far north of Scotland. In spite of past attempts to introduce this bird into Ireland it has never established itself in that country. In the rest of Europe the tawny owl is widespread as far north as central Norway and Sweden and it is said to be increasing its range in southern Finland. Elsewhere it is to be found throughout Europe and as far south as the Atlas region of North Africa. Eastwards its range extends through Asia Minor, the Himalayan region and north-west India to southern China.

The British population of tawny owls appears to have remained stable throughout this century and if anything its numbers have increased slightly. The bird has maintained itself in the face of man's impact upon its environment because it is evidently tolerant of human presence and is able to adjust its diet to the food available. The success of the tawny owl may have been a contributory factor in the decline of the long-eared owl (*Asio otus*) in Britain, possibly as a result of direct competition for food and living space. In Britain the principal habitat of the tawny owl is broadleaved and mixed woodland but in other parts of Europe coniferous forests are also inhabited. The bird's adaptability to varying lifestyles is reflected in some of the other habitats it occupies in Britain and elsewhere, for example open farmland, old gardens, church yards, city centre parks and squares. In some parts of northern Scotland it also inhabits quite open moorland.

The tawny owl is very largely nocturnal and is rarely active during daylight hours. At dawn the bird will return to its roosting site which may be a derelict or infrequently occupied building. More usually a cavity in a tree is used or else any tree providing good cover, for example yew, holly or any ivy clad tree. In the latter case the bird perches on a large branch with its side against the trunk and its colouration camouflages it. It is extremely difficult to approach a roosting tawny owl without the bird becoming aware of one's presence. So acute is its hearing that the bird will turn to face an intruder at the slightest sound and stare.

If a roosting tawny owl is discovered by a small bird such as a chaffinch, the latter will utter its alarm call, hopping from branch to branch often within a yard of the owl. Other birds including the robin, wren, blackbird, tits and sometimes the magpie and jay are attracted by the sound and join the incessant mobbing. The owl merely faces the intruders and never attacks under such circumstances. At length it may take off and fly perhaps a hundred yards or so to another favourite perch in the hope of avoiding the mobbers. The significance of this mobbing behaviour is not easy to explain. Tawny owls very rarely seem to hunt by day so the alarm calls do not broadcast the presence of an active predator on the hunt. It would seem unlikely that occasional mobbing would ever result in an owl abandoning its territory and moving elsewhere. Possibly mobbing helps to reinforce the owl's nocturnal lifestyle so that it tends to hunt only when the other birds are roosting and therefore more secure from predation.

As with many species of owl, pellet analysis can and has yielded a good deal of information about the diet of this species. In this way about 20 types of mammal have been identified as food of the tawny owl, the more usual prey being voles, mice, shrews, rats and young rabbits. Others identified include the mole, the weasel, the grey squirrel and certain types of bat. Around 40 bird species have been recorded, ranging in size from the goldcrest to the pheasant. Presumably these are taken either when active at dawn and dusk or else at the roosting site. Incubating birds are perhaps taken to some extent. It is of interest to note that captive tawny owls occasionally store food and moreover remember where they have hidden it.

Whether this is a practice of wild birds appears to be uncertain. Food is sometimes stored at the nest when the young are satiated.

About 90 per cent of the vertebrate diet of woodland owls appears to be mammals and the remainder is birds. In contrast, the situation is reversed in those owls living in city centre parks where small mammals are relatively scarce. In addition to mammals and birds, earthworms form an important part of the diet and beetles, snails and slugs appear to be eaten to a lesser extent. To this end tawny owls can and do walk and run well on the ground. There have even been reports of birds taking small, surface swimming fish. The results of some detailed studies on the diet of tawny owls are described in a later chapter.

With its excellent vision and acute hearing the tawny owl is well equipped to hunt in darkness. Its technique is to drop stone-like, spreading its wings only at the last moment in order to brake and then cover the prey which is seized with the claws and crushed. By relying on its sense of hearing the tawny owl can hunt in almost total darkness. At such times its silent flight allows it to locate and follow prey without noisy wing-beats which might interfere with its hearing or disturb the prey.

Tawny owls hoot at all times of the year, usually from some vantage point but occasionally when in flight. However they are at their most vocal between October and December since this is the period when territories are established. Woodland tawny owls are said to be more vocal than those occupying more open country. This could be because there is more competition for the prime woodland territories. One study in Britain showed woodland territories to be about 24 to 28 hectares in size and indicated that these are quite exclusive, boundaries being strictly observed.

Not surprisingly courtship in this nocturnal species is more often heard than seen. In addition to the hoot and 'ke-wick' calls mentioned earlier, a variety of loud, harsh barks and screeches are associated with this event. The male will display to the female using a variety of swaying and bobbing movements together with wing raising and puffing up and flattening his feathers. The female responds by similarly raising and lowering her feathers and by rapid quivering. Breeding generally begins in earnest in March; there is just one brood raised in a year. The usual nest site is a cavity within a tree, generally less than 7.5 metres from the ground,

Tawny owl in flight; the slotted nature of the primary feathers and their fur-like trailing edges can be seen clearly. Compare with photo on p.28 and Fig.5

although nests much higher than this are not unusual. Alternative nest sites are quite varied and include old nests of for example the magpie, the crow or the grey squirrel. Old or little occupied buildings are sometimes used and the birds will take to suitable nest-boxes. Tawny owls will occasionally nest upon the ground, for example in the entrance to a rabbit burrow. Ground nesting is not uncommon in the thinly wooded parts of its range in the Scottish highlands.

No nest material is used and the almost spherical, pure white eggs are laid at intervals of anything from two to seven days. The completed clutch is usually two to four eggs although more are laid occasionally. The average clutch size varies from year to year with the abundance of food; a well nourished female is able to lay more eggs than one enduring a food shortage. Incubation is carried out by the female and begins as soon as the first egg is laid. Consequently the eggs hatch at different times resulting in a brood of chicks of varied ages and sizes. Each egg requires about 29 days incubation but the total incubation period can be appreciably longer than this if a number of eggs are laid at fairly widely spaced intervals. During this period the male will bring food to the female.

The young remain in the nest for anything between 27 and 35 days. The female stays with them and all rely upon the male for food. Normally he has a definite landing site near the nest to which he brings the prey. In response to calls from the male, the female will leave the nest to collect the food but if the young are small or the night is cold she will often not do so and the male then takes the food to the nest. This is the one time of year when hard-pressed tawny owls may hunt in daylight, after dawn following a short summer night. If necessary the female will defend her young fiercely and persons approaching the nest of this species have been known to receive serious head and face injuries.

Having left the nest the young owls remain dependent upon their parents for some time. A study of one family of owls indicated this period to be about three months. This suggests that the young owls have a lot to learn before they can lead an independent existence. Hunting behaviour is probably basically instinctive but presumably there is a large learnt component; the innate skill must be perfected. Having reached independence, each young owl must then seek out and establish a territory during its first autumn.

LONG-EARED OWL (*Asio otus*)

This is a medium sized brown owl which is nocturnal and inhabits woodland and forests, having a preference for conifers. Its scientific name means long-eared owl and in Britain two other names for this bird are the horned owl and the tufted owl. All these names obviously refer to its most striking feature, the large and normally conspicuous ear tufts. Of the European owls only the eagle owl has ear tufts of a proportionately similar size and it is a bird twice the size of the long-eared owl.

The upper-parts of the long-eared owl are barred and mottled with dark brown and buff, the wings having buff or white fringes to the coverts. The under-parts are paler, generally a light grey-brown or buff, with dark brown streaks and fine bars. The facial disc is normally a yellowish buff colour, shading to black around the eyes which are orange-yellow. Pale feathering slants upwards from either side of the dark bill to points above each eye giving the impression of frowning eyebrows. The ear tufts are each made up of six narrow feathers which are dark brown in the centre and edged with buff. When seen in flight the lower surface of the wings are pale with a dark carpal or wrist patch. The long-eared owl is about 355 mm long and adults can weigh anything between 245 and 400 grammes, weight varying seasonally and being at a maximum in spring and autumn.

This is a very widespread species and is to be found throughout the northern hemisphere between latitudes 30°N and 60°N up to an altitude of at least 2,100 metres. It is resident in all parts of the British Isles although it is more abundant in Scotland, northern England and Ireland. It is also resident in southern and central Europe but populations in northern Europe are migratory and move south or west in winter, some to the British Isles and others to areas around the Mediterranean. Within Britain there may be some southward movement in winter. These birds are known to migrate in flocks and groups have been observed on passage over the Shetland Islands, the Orkneys and along the coast of north-east England. Flocks have also been seen crossing some of the high Swiss passes, for example the Col de Bretolet.

Although primarily a woodland bird, the long-eared owl is sometimes to be found in more open habitats such as heather moor, scrub or parkland. However, unlike the tawny owl, it avoids city parks and human habitations in general. For this reason and because it is a strictly nocturnal species, the long-eared owl is easily overlooked in areas where it occurs and it has been studied less than many other European owl species.

By day the long-eared owl will roost in a tree, either an evergreen or some other tree providing dense cover, for example one which is ivy clad. The bird will perch close to the trunk, where its bark-coloured plumage renders it well camouflaged. In open areas these birds will roost in gorse or bramble or even on the ground amid long grass. Communal roosts are not at all uncommon outside the breeding season, a feature which is unusual among European owl species. Such roosts may include up to 20 birds and in some instances it has been known for each bird to have a particular perch to which it returned every day. When undisturbed and relaxed, roosting long-eared owls have their plumage fluffed up, the facial discs partially closed and the ear tufts lowered flat along the top of the head. But when aroused, for example by an approaching person, they adopt a strikingly different appearance; the feathers are pulled close to the body making the bird appear upright and slender. At such times they remain quite motionless and do not constantly turn to face an intruder as does the tawny owl. With their cryptic plumage this renders the long-eared owl very difficult to see, the resemblance to a broken branch being considerable. On adopting this posture, the ear tufts are raised possibly as a warning signal to other individuals in the roost and the facial disc is opened presumably so that the intruder can be tracked by sound. It is possible to approach to within a few feet of a roosting long-eared owl if care is taken. Eventually the bird will take flight, manoeuvring silently and expertly through the trees as it moves off in search of an alternative resting place.

As with many owl species the diet can vary with locality and the availability of prey. One study carried out in the Scottish highlands in an area of pines and open moorland showed that the composition of the diet varied on a seasonal basis. In March, short-tailed voles made up about 54 per cent by weight of the diet and a further 21 per cent consisted of wood mice. Fewer wood mice were taken during autumn, when they accounted for only three per cent of the food intake. At this season the chief prey were the short-tailed vole (48 per cent) and the bank vole (14 per cent). Broadly similar dietary patterns have been demonstrated in other parts of Europe, with voles being the most important prey item and birds normally making up only a small part of the diet. However in Ireland where the long-eared owl is widespread and the short-tailed vole absent, the diet is rather different. Here the brown rat is the chief prey species, making up about 20 per cent by weight of the food taken. A wide variety of species have been recorded as occasional prey of the long-eared owl, including bats, lizards, snakes, frogs, toads and some insects. Curiously shrews appear to be eaten very rarely, a feature which contrasts with the diet of many other European owls. These mammals are readily taken by the barn, tawny and short-eared owls. Birds noted in the diet usually include finches, thrushes and starlings whilst predation upon sparrows appears to be a British peculiarity for some unknown reason. More unusual avian prey recorded are the jay, swallow and goldcrest. Intriguingly the list also includes the blue tit, great tit and willow tit, birds which all roost in tree cavities; consequently it would be of great interest to know when and how such species are caught.

The regurgitated pellets of the long-eared owl are grey and about 35 to 65 mm long and 15 to 25 mm in diameter, being similar to those of the tawny owl in their appearance and friable consistency. The long-eared owl is not without its own predators, for in Europe it can fall prey to the much larger eagle owl.

Experiments have shown that the long-eared owl is capable of locating and catching prey in total darkness. This indicates that hearing is likely to be of considerable importance to this owl when hunting. Small mammals are probably caught near forest and woodland edges whilst birds are known to be taken from their roosting sites, a feat which must require great skill in flight control on the part of the owl. There have been reports of pairs of long-eared owls hunting for birds along hedgerows. In such circumstances one owl flies alongside the hedge flushing out roosting birds while the second owl flies silently along the other side to catch any small bird that takes flight. It would be interesting to know how food is subsequently shared in such a partnership.

Courtship takes place from the end of the year until March and this is the time when the long-eared owl is most often heard calling. The hoot is quiet but carries well and can be described as a 'poop-poop-poop-poop', not unlike the noise made by blowing across the top of an empty bottle. In addition a barking call is sometimes uttered at this time of year. There is a courtship flight in which the bird flies slowly with deep wing-beats occasionally clapping the wings beneath the body.

The long-eared owl generally lays its eggs in the old nest of another species. Nests used include those of raptors, jays, herons and wood pigeons whilst even the drey of a squirrel is used occasionally. Such a nest may be from a height of 15 metres in coniferous or deciduous trees down to one metre or so in gorse. Long-eared owls living in open habitats will nest upon the ground. This occurs in mountainous parts of their range in central Europe and also upon the heather moors of the Orkney Islands. In the south of the long-eared owl's range nesting activity generally begins in March or early April but in the north the start is later.

As with most species of owl reproductive success is dependent upon the availability of food, and in particular rodents. The number of breeding pairs in an area, the number of clutches produced, clutch size and fledging success are all affected by food supply. Consequently the number of eggs laid is variable, there normally being just one clutch of four or five eggs, but in years when food is abundant up to ten eggs may be laid. At such times it

Long-eared owls occupying open habitats will nest on the ground, but elsewhere it is more usual for them to take over abandoned nests of birds such as raptors

is possible that a second brood may be raised although there do not appear to be any certain records of this. The eggs are almost spherical and white, incubation beginning as soon as the first has been laid. On average they require about 27 days incubation by the female before hatching takes place.

It is apparently unusual for all the eggs to hatch and highly unusual for all the chicks which do hatch to survive until they fledge. At first the young are white but later the down becomes barred with grey brown. Fledging occurs when they are about three weeks old, from early June onwards. At this period the juveniles are quite noisy, having a squeaking hunger call which is sometimes made by day as well as by night. Even when the young are eventually able to fly they remain dependent upon their parents for some time.

The long-eared owl will display aggressively if an intruder enters its breeding territory. The display is similar to that of the short-eared owl, the secondary wing feathers being arched upwards over the back and the primaries spread out.

In Britain the long-eared owl has declined in numbers during the twentieth century, especially in England and Wales. It had already become scarce in many areas by the 1930s. Over the same period much marginal land was cleared for agricultural use and it is likely that this was the pertinent factor in the decline of this species. There has been no marked fall in numbers in Ireland where such agricultural changes have taken place to a lesser extent. In Northumberland, the Lake District and the Wigtown area of south-west Scotland the long-eared owl appears to have declined in numbers while the tawny owl has increased. The absence of the latter species from Ireland may prevent such possible 'replacement' occurring. In Denmark the long-eared owl has benefited from the widespread planting of coniferous trees. Hopefully this practice will be of similar value to these birds in Britain and their decline in numbers will be reversed in the future.

SHORT-EARED OWL (*Asio flammeus*)

The common name of this owl is somewhat surprising since its ear tufts are very small and difficult to see in the field. Its scientific name is if anything more puzzling; *Asio* is Latin for long-eared owl and *flammeus* means flame-coloured from the Latin *flamma* for flame, yet this owl is a mottled brown colour. In Britain the only alternative common name used to any extent is the woodcock owl. It was so named because many wintering short-eared owls arrive at about the same time as the woodcock.

The range of the short-eared owl is worldwide. In the northern hemisphere it occurs in a circumpolar band between latitudes 40°N and 70°N including most of northern and central Europe. It is also found in many parts of South America and on many island groups, for example Hawaii, the Galapagos Islands and the West Indies. Not surprisingly with this very large range some eight subspecies or races have been described, but only one of these, *Asio flammeus flammeus*, occurs in Europe. In the British Isles the short-eared owl is a resident breeding species in Scotland, northern England as far south as Yorkshire, and north Wales. It is also resident in south-west Wales and along coastal areas of eastern England. In autumn the British population is increased by the arrival of European immigrants and in winter it is a much more common and widespread species. At this season it can be seen in areas of suitable habitat throughout the British Isles. In Ireland this species occurs as a winter visitor only. During winter there is some southward movement of Scottish birds to coastal areas and other suitable places in England.

This is a medium-sized owl with relatively long wings when compared with other owl species of a similar size, the wingspan being about one metre. This latter feature is testimony to its open habitat and nomadic tendencies, for this species is much more aerial than for example the blunt-winged tawny owl. Female short-eared owls are on average larger than the males. An adult female is about 420 mm long and the male is about 360 mm. Weight varies a good deal from one individual to another and on a seasonal basis. A female can weigh anything from 280 to 390 grammes and a male 200 to 360 grammes. This bird normally rests on the ground, adopting a somewhat horizontal posture which is uncharacteristic of owls. Only rarely does it perch in a bush or tree.

The short eared owl is generally a pale buff colour below, streaked with dark brown. The upper parts are mottled with the same two colours, the overall appearance being darker above. When in flight it has noticeable dark carpal or wrist patches on both the upper and lower surfaces of the wings and also a yellowish trailing edge to the wing. At reasonably close range the eyes can be seen. These are a striking lemon yellow and help distinguish it from the long-eared owl which has orange eyes and of course much larger ear tufts, although these are not always readily apparent. The only other medium-sized brown owl in Britain is the tawny owl and this lacks ear tufts and has large, dark eyes. The short-eared owl has generally pale facial discs becoming dark around the eyes. The bill and also the claws are black, the legs being feathered to the feet.

The short-eared owl is most active around dawn and dusk but it is often to be encountered by day since it is one of the most diurnal of European owls. In contrast the tawny and long-eared owls are strictly nocturnal in their habits. The short-eared owl roosts in grass cover, often on sloping ground where there is a good view of at least some of the surrounding area. This is not a bird of arable land but one of open, rough grassland and heath. Young conifer plantations are also frequented since these are suitable areas for its chief prey, the short-tailed vole. But once the young trees grow to a point where the underlying grass cover disappears this habitat is no longer suitable.

The food of this owl is generally small mammals of a variety of species, principally the short-tailed vole and also the bank vole, water vole, brown rat and shrew species. Squirrels have also been recorded as an item of diet, which is fairly surprising in view of the open habitat occupied by the short-eared owl. Birds generally form a minor part of the diet, the species taken usually being small ones, but black-headed gull, lapwing, hoopoe and jackdaw have been recorded. One study conducted in the Outer Hebrides from April to September indicated that 63 per cent by weight of the diet was made up of voles and 31 per cent consisted of brown rats. However, many cases of variation from the above pattern have been noted, for example in 1939 a bird in Wales was found to have been subsisting upon a diet of about 50 per cent rabbit and 33 per cent birds, including knot, snipe, dunlin and sanderling. T. A. Coward described the short-eared owl taking birds on the wing when migrating, the owls apparently seeing them on misty nights in the glare from lighthouses. In the northern part of its European range the short-eared owl is migratory. This is not surprising because many of the small mammal species upon which it feeds hibernate and those that do not are able to move about beneath a protective layer of snow, relatively safe from predators.

The hunting technique of this owl appears casual; the bird flies low, gliding and manoeuvring with the wings shallowly inclined. Having located suitable prey, such as a vole, on the ground, it drops quickly. In contrast, when the birds are migrating their line of flight is direct and the slow, rhythmic wing-beats give the appearance of considerable strength. There is also a courtship flight, sometimes performed at surprisingly great heights. During these the bird circles with the wings held quite stiffly and calls in bursts of about 10 to 20 short notes best described as a deep 'boo-boo-boo'. It then drops vertically, clapping the wings below the body perhaps four or five times. After the bird has regained its original height the performance is repeated. Apart from the note described above, the short-eared owl is generally a silent bird. It will utter a harsh, barking call if an intruder enters its territory.

Short-eared owl with two small owlets and three eggs still to hatch

The territory is some six to eight hectares or more and in suitable areas of habitat there may be up to about six breeding pairs per square kilometre. Although this bird and its near relative the long-eared owl normally inhabit rather different areas, the latter being a bird of woodland and woodland edges, the two have been found nesting as little as 30 metres apart in Finland. Apparently the birds tolerated each other's presence without harm to either pair. In continental Europe relationships between other owl species are not always so amicable.

The nest is on the ground, usually in a grassy hollow. Food supply greatly influences breeding and in a year when voles are abundant from seven to ten eggs may be laid (up to fourteen have been recorded). However, in years when food supply is poor the clutch size is more likely to be three to six. In a good year breeding may begin in March and there can be two clutches, but in Britain the first egg is normally laid in late April or early May and at this point incubation begins. Subsequent eggs are laid at two-day intervals. This is the typical pattern in owl reproduction, resulting in a brood of varying sizes and ages. In the short-eared owl early incubation is generally not continuous so the first eggs laid take longer to incubate and the gap in the ages of the chicks is not as large as might be expected from the intervals between egg laying.

71

Short-eared owl with offspring at typical ground nest site

The average incubation period for an egg is about 28 days. This species will defend its territory against human intruders and will dive at and sometimes strike a person who approaches the nest.

When newly hatched the chicks have down feathers which have white tips and are either dark grey or barred at the base, the result being an over-all dirty white appearance. The young spend the first two weeks of life in the nest but during the following three weeks or so they begin to explore and gradually move up to about 100 metres away from the nest site. At this stage they are quite vociferous, making loud squeaks as they beg for food brought to them by the parents. If approached they will puff up their feathers and snap their bills in defence. As they become older the young tend to wander further away and very gradually they become independent of their parents.

It has long been known that the population of short-eared owls in an area is limited to a very large extent by the numbers of prey animals available. Since populations of small mammals are liable to large fluctuations so too are the numbers of short-eared owls within a particular area. The following description is to be found in Holinshed's *Chronicles of England, Scotland and Ireland* and relates a vole plague on the Southminster marshes in Essex during 1580. 'There suddenly appeared a multitude of mice which overwhelmed the marshes, shearing and gnawing the grass and so spoiling and tainting it that the cattle grazing it were smitten with a murrain and died. Man could not destroy them but finally more owls than could have existed in the whole county flocked to the marshes and so the marsh holders were delivered from their plague of mice.'

In a young conifer plantation in Scotland about 35 pairs of short-eared owls nested within an area of about 13 km² during the summers of 1953 and 1954. At this time the vole population of the area was very large. In May 1954 the number of voles began to decline rapidly and by June there were very few. Subsequently only two pairs of owls remained, each with territories about ten times the size of those held previously.

In this way it appears that the short-eared owl is very dependent upon the abundance of suitable prey. If food becomes scarce, breeding performance is adversely affected and the birds will move elsewhere. This strategy of movement at least gives the birds a chance of finding another area where there is enough food to sustain them. In contrast, the tawny owl will not move out of its woodland territory during periods of food shortage. The probable reason for this is that the tawny owl builds up a detailed knowledge of the vegetation and hunting areas within its physically and biologically more complex and varied territory. To move elsewhere would mean that the bird would be giving up a considerable advantage for it would undoubtedly be a less efficient hunter in unfamiliar territory. The habitat of the short-eared owl is much more uniform and successful hunting is presumably less dependent upon local knowledge. For this species there is evidently more to be gained than lost by moving when food is short.

4 European owls not resident in Britain

SCOPS OWL (*Otus scops*)

This bird is a small, brownish owl often seen in trees close to human habitation. However, among European owls it is unique in having a breeding distribution limited to the southern half of the continent. Its common name is probably derived from the Greek *skopeo*, meaning to look at, referring to its large, staring eyes. The scops owl is one of 35 species placed within the genus *Otus*, this being about a quarter of all living owl species. Surprisingly it is the only representative of this group to be found in Europe, many of the *Otus* species being tropical in distribution.

The scops owl is approximately 190 mm in length and gives the impression of small size because it is a slim bird with a proportionately small head for an owl. The upper-parts are a greyish brown shading to a more tawny colour on the sides, all being finely barred and streaked with dark brown. Across the scapulars of each wing there is a line of off-white markings. The under-parts are a light grey-brown, again marked with dark brown in the form of narrow streaks and very fine, wavy barring. The tail is barred with off-white and grey, and the unfeathered toes are grey. The scops owl has an indistinct facial disc which is grey-brown, shading to a reddish brown around the edges and around the eyes which are proportionately large and bright yellow. The bill is dark brown and there is a dark border on the lower edge of the facial disc. Apart from its small size one of the chief distinguishing features of the scops owl is the presence of small ear tufts. However when the bird is at rest these are lowered and are not particularly conspicuous.

This species can be distinguished from the similar-sized little owl by its apparently smaller head, the presence of ear tufts and a somewhat longer tail. The flight path of the scops owl is direct, contrasting with the undulating flight of the little owl.

Scops owl returning to its nest

In Europe, the scops owl occurs as a breeding species south of about latitude 47°N, including Portugal, Spain, the southern half of France, Italy, Yugoslavia, Greece and the Balkan countries. Elsewhere it is to be found in the Atlas region of North Africa, Turkey and parts of southern and western U.S.S.R. There is a separate population in southern and eastern Asia but some authorities have ranked this as a distinct species, *Otus sunia*.

During autumn European scops owls move southwards to winter in the Mediterranean region and central Africa. They have been recorded as vagrants in many of the countries in northern Europe including Britain, Norway and Sweden. In the British Isles this species has been sighted on about 70 occasions although there have been relatively fewer records during recent years. Birds have generally been seen in either spring or autumn at localities throughout the country.

The scops owl is nocturnal and by day it roosts in typical owl fashion perched in a tree close to the trunk where it is well camouflaged. When it becomes aware of a human intruder the behaviour of this species is remarkably similar to that of the long-eared owl. It stands motionless and erect, flattens its body plumage and raises its ear tufts. The general habitat of scops owls is open areas with trees, often near human habitation, for example gardens, orchards, parks and hedgerows containing trees.

As might be guessed from the migratory habits of this owl, its diet consists almost entirely of insects, in particular beetles, moths, grasshoppers and crickets. Some mammals are taken occasionally, such as mice or shrews, and also a variety of small birds. Most hunting takes place either shortly after sunset or during the hours just prior to sunrise. Where their ranges overlap, the scops owl can fall prey to the larger tawny owl, possibly as a result of competition for suitable nest sites.

The call made by the scops owl is a short, musical but monotonous whistle of two syllables variously described as 'pew', 'tyeu' or 'kiou'. This is repeated at about three-second intervals, sometimes for hours on end. Both the male and the female make this call but the note of the latter is said to be higher pitched, longer and more distinctly of two syllables. During the warm spring nights of southern Europe a highly similar call is made by another quite different animal, the midwife toad, *Alytes obstetricans*. Correctly identifying a caller as owl or toad is not at all easy.

At the onset of the breeding season pairs of scops owls are inclined to spend more time in the vicinity of the nest site. This is usually a tree cavity, often in an olive tree or cork oak. Occasionally suitable holes in walls or other masonry are used and sometimes the abandoned nest of another bird such as the magpie is taken over.

Not surprisingly, with the dietary emphasis upon insects, breeding performance in this owl does not fluctuate with population changes of small mammals. From three to six eggs are laid, usually four or five. These are about 32 mm in length, being somewhat rounded, white and slightly glossy. In Europe most clutches are laid during the first two weeks of May but laying can commence as early as mid April or as late as the beginning of June. Only the female incubates the eggs which hatch after about 24 days. During this time and when the chicks are small, the male provides all the food required, but as the nestlings grow the female starts to leave them on occasions to take part in hunting. The young fledge after about three weeks or a little more but like most owl species their power of flight is poor for the first few days. There is no characteristic juvenile plumage and the young birds, once fully grown, are very similar in appearance to the adults.

EAGLE OWL (*Bubo bubo*)

This is Europe's largest owl, being 660 to 710 mm long with a wingspan of 1.6 to 1.8 metres. It is predominantly brown and has ear tufts which are over 50 mm long. In Europe only the great grey and Ural owls are of a similar size and colour but both of these species lack ear tufts. The female eagle owl is larger than the male, the difference in weight being greater than that in overall length; females weigh 3 to 3.5 kg and males 2 to 3 kg. Size apart, the sexes are similar in appearance. The upper-parts are dark brown, mottled with orange-buff, the wings and tail being barred. The under-parts are a pale buff streaked with dark brown. On the breast these markings are relatively broad whilst on the lower breast and belly they are finer and there is also some barring. The legs and feet are clad in mottled brown feathers, the claws being black. The bill is dark brown. The brilliant orange eyes are a striking feature of the eagle owl. Referring to the closely related Magellanic eagle owl (a race of the great horned owl, *Bubo virginanus*, found in Patagonia), Hudson described these as, 'great globes of quivering yellow flame, the black pupils being surrounded by a scintillating crimson light which [throws] out minute yellow sparks into the air'.

The eagle owl is found in many parts of Europe although it is uncommon in all but a few areas. It is absent from Britain and the north-west of Europe in general, including northern France, Belgium, the Netherlands and northern Germany. Outside Europe it occurs in North Africa and throughout much of Asia, approximately between latitudes 10°N and 65°N which includes the Indian subcontinent.

The eagle owl is the only European owl species to have suffered extensively from persecution by man, for up until the early twentieth century it was widely regarded as vermin and suitable quarry by hunters. For example, in Norway 1,359 birds were shot

Nestling eagle owls

between 1908 and 1915 for state-paid bounties. By 1960 only about 600 pairs of eagle owls remained in that country but since then the species has been afforded legal protection during the breeding season. The eagle owl is now a protected species throughout most of Europe but regrettably the enforcement of such laws is not always an easy matter.

In recent years the eagle owl has recovered to a small extent, partly as a result of natural recolonization of former strongholds, as for example in the Baden-Württemberg area of West Germany where the original population of perhaps 200 pairs was reduced to extinction by 1930. By 1978 there were about 12 pairs in this area. Artificial reintroduction schemes have also been successful, as in the Kilsbergen mountains in Sweden where the national population fell dramatically during the nineteenth and early twentieth centuries to an estimated 455 pairs by 1948 and only 175 pairs by 1965. Some of the birds involved in this reintroduction scheme and a similar one in the Eifel area of northern West Germany were bred at the Norfolk Wildlife Park in Britain. The procedure was to establish breeding eagle owls in aviaries in the areas concerned. These birds were retained whilst their offspring were allowed freedom of movement, eventually becoming independent.

The eagle owl is a bird of open woodland in low, mountainous areas up to an altitude of about 4,500 metres in Europe. It is a very solitary species and even during the breeding season there is relatively little contact between the individuals of a pair. The territory may be from five to ten km in diameter depending upon the abundance of food. Within it there are usually several breeding sites which are used in approximate rotation by the occupying pair of birds since the same pair will often retain a particular territory for several years. The eagle owl is sedentary in its habits although a small number of birds may wander outside the breeding season and some mountain populations move to lower altitudes in winter.

The eagle owl calls most frequently during December and January prior to breeding. The hoot is a continuous 'ooohu-ooohu-ooohu'; the scientific name for this species, *Bubo bubo*, stems from the Greek *buzo*, to hoot. Other sounds made by this species include a wide variety of moaning, grating and rattling noises. In central Europe a pair of eagle owls will take up a nest site in late February or early March. The nest is a shallow depression in the ground containing a few leaves, typically among rocks in the uppermost regions of a river valley from where there is a good view of the surrounding area. Alternative sites include tree cavities and old nests of various raptors. Two to four white eggs about 60 mm long and 50 mm in diameter are laid during late March or April, incubation taking about 35 days per egg. The eggs hatch at two-day intervals. Except in unusual circumstances the male supplies all the food for the young. There is usually a food station near the nest to which the male takes prey for the female to collect; however, the male will occasionally take food directly to the nest. The young disperse after about seven weeks but initially their power of flight is poor.

The diet of the eagle owl is highly varied, a fact well illustrated by one study carried out in Sweden. Based upon 484 prey items, it indicated that the diet consisted of 18 per cent brown rat, 18 per cent other rodents (voles, mice and lemmings), 9 per cent hooded crow, 9 per cent game birds, 8 per cent hedgehog, 7 per cent red squirrel, 5 per cent duck, 4 per cent hare and numerous other species. In all, the diet comprised 55 per cent mammals, 33 per cent birds, 11 per cent fish and 1 per cent reptiles and amphibians. The largest prey species noted were capercaillie, buzzard, goshawk, osprey and wildcat. In other studies a variety of owl species have been noted in the diet, including the long-eared owl, tawny owl, Tengmalm's owl, little owl, hawk owl and even the snowy owl. This suggests that the eagle owl is intolerant of the presence of other owl species within its territory and removes at least some birds by the simple expedient of predation.

In Britain the eagle owl was probably not an uncommon visitor to the far north around 200 years ago, since during the first quarter of the nineteenth century Thomas Bewick wrote of it, 'The eagle owl is one of the largest of the British owls . . . . . sometimes met with in the northern Scottish isles where it feeds upon rabbits and grouse but it is very rarely seen in England.' It is tempting to speculate that this species may have been resident in Scotland when it was still extensively forested during the period following the last glaciation. The last reliable record of an eagle owl sighted in Britain dates from 1883. More recent sightings have been reported but the birds concerned may have been of captive origin.

HAWK OWL (*Surnia ulula*)

The hawk owl is a medium-sized owl of about 360 to 410 mm in length, though this measurement is somewhat misleading since the tail of this species is comparatively much longer than that of any other European owl. The hawk owl is well named since in many ways it resembles a hawk in its appearance and is quite diurnal in its habits. It is a bird of thinly wooded areas such as forest clearings, and in Europe its breeding distribution is limited to Scandinavia, Finland and European U.S.S.R.

The upper-parts are grey-brown, thickly mottled with white, the tail being barred with grey-brown and white. Below, this bird is an off-white colour with densely packed, fine, grey-brown barring; a very hawk-like feature. The facial disc is pale grey shading to a dark grey around the eyes which are bright yellow and small in size. The bill is a pale yellow and beneath it is a small, dark grey bib. The facial disc is bordered with dark grey feathers and is incomplete, not extending above the eyes. There are no ear tufts and the head has a somewhat flat-topped appearance.

This owl is hawk-like not only in aspects of its plumage but also in its behaviour. It perches in a much less upright position than do more typical owls, often with the long tail pointing upwards. Occasionally while at rest the hawk owl will raise its tail and then lower it again slowly. It does not have the dense plumage of most owls and the feathers of the short pointed wings are virtually lacking in any sound deadening filaments. The ear openings in the skull of this species are relatively small and symmetrically

9. *Short-eared owl with prey; its lemon-yellow eyes are a*
striking feature

10. *Scops owl; the delicately marked plumage of this small*
owl form excellent camouflage

11. Eagle owl with prey

12. Hawk owl; its heavily barred underparts are a noticeable feature

13. *Pygmy owl; the disproportionately large legs and feet of Europe's smallest owl allow it to take prey equal to its own weight*
14. *Female Ural owl; this species is similar in appearance to, though larger than, the tawny owl*

15. Great grey owl with distinctive concentric markings on its facial disc

16. Tengmalm's owl

Female hawk owl on nest

positioned, both features indicating a probable lack of reliance upon hearing when the bird is hunting.

Within Europe the hawk owl is to be found in central and northern Sweden and Norway, throughout most of Finland and in northern U.S.S.R. From here it occurs in a wide band across Asia to the Pacific coast, the northern limit of its range coinciding with the northern tree limit at about 65°N. However where there are trees in more northerly latitudes, for example in sheltered river valleys, this owl may be found associated with them. In the U.S.S.R. the southern limit of its range coincides with the change from forest to steppe country. The hawk owl also occurs in Canada and Alaska where it is deemed to be a distinct subspecies, *Surnia ulula caparoch*. The Eurasian bird is named *Surnia ulula ulula*.

The hawk owl is generally sedentary but some individuals tend to move southwards during winter especially when food is hard to find. It occurs as a vagrant in parts of Poland and Germany during most winters and is occasionally recorded as far south as Switzerland and other central European countries. This owl is a very rare visitor to Britain. There are eight early records dating from the period 1830 to 1903, some of these birds apparently being the American subspecies. More recent sightings include one bird at Gurnards Head, near St. Ives in Cornwall, on 14 August 1966 and another near Chipping in Lancashire on 13 September 1959. In all, these records are from widely scattered localities and the older records are mostly for the months of November and December.

The hawk owl is a bird of thinly wooded areas and favours forest clearings especially amid larch or mixed larch and birch. It is also occasionally found in parkland and other similar areas.

The diet consists very largely of voles during the summer months, with lemmings, small birds and insects taken only occasionally. In winter however its feeding habits become much more diverse and at this time of year voles account for only about 40 per cent of the food intake. A further 33 per cent consists of birds of a variety of species. Willow grouse are important and there are reports of hawk owls following flocks of these birds, and also ptarmigan, during times of deep snow when mammalian prey is difficult to locate. These birds are almost as large as the hawk owl itself which is testimony to its prowess as a hunter.

The hawk owl is a diurnal bird, being most active during the daylight hours of early morning and late evening. Hunting is generally carried out from a vantage point in a tree but the hawk owl will sometimes seek out prey in true hawk-like fashion, flying rapidly and close to the ground. They are able to catch birds on the wing. In addition the hawk owl can hover competently when the need arises. Although not a small bird and quite fearless in the presence of man, this owl does occasionally fall prey to larger species such as the eagle owl.

Courtship in the hawk owl includes a display flight performed by the male. During this he flies above the tree tops of his territory, occasionally clapping his wings and calling. This call is a soft, musical and frequently repeated 'poo-poo-poo-poo'. In addition, during early spring the male will utter a whistling call which can be described as 'wita-wita-wita-wita'.

Nesting can begin as early as February, depending upon latitude and the prevailing weather conditions. The nest site is normally a tree cavity, often in the top of a broken conifer trunk. Abandoned nests of birds such as the carrion crow and magpie are also taken over upon occasions, possibly in territories where no suitable cavity is available. In the tree cavity sites, nesting material is sometimes employed, usually twigs, moss or fragments of wood from the hole itself. A lining of feathers is often added. As stated above, hawk owls rely heavily upon voles as a source of food during the summer months and breeding performance is very dependent upon the abundance of these mammals during any particular year. Normally three to six eggs are laid but up to nine may be produced in years when there is a plentiful supply of food. The largest clutch ever recorded for this species was 13 eggs. April and May are the normal months during which the clutch is completed but later dates in the northern part of the range and earlier ones in the south are not uncommon.

Unusually for owls both sexes may take part in incubation but the female always assumes the major role in this activity which begins as soon as the first egg has been laid. Each egg requires about 28 days incubation before hatching takes place. The young are at first clad in short, white down but after about a month the juvenile plumage begins to develop. This is a pale brown on the under-parts and a darker rusty brown on the upper-parts. The white spotting and barring is much more sparse than in the adults.

The hawk owl is considered to be sufficiently different from other owl species to be placed within a genus of its own. The generic name *Surnia* appears to have no known derivation whilst *ulula*, its specific name, is Latin for screech owl.

EURASIAN PYGMY OWL (*Glaucidium passerinum*)

The Eurasian pygmy owl is a bird not frequently seen by the casual observer and it appears to have been less studied than many of Europe's owl species. This is probably due to several factors including its small size, generally nocturnal habits and the fact that its range is restricted to thickly forested areas of northern and central Europe where it is sparsely distributed. Only 165 mm long, this diminutive bird is Europe's smallest owl and its near relative the least pygmy owl, *Glaucidium minutissimum*, is the smallest owl species in the world. The least pygmy owl inhabits parts of Mexico and South America and is just 120 mm long.

The Eurasian pygmy owl has brown upper-parts spotted with pale buff whilst the under-parts are light grey and streaked with dark brown. The head is proportionately small, flat-topped in appearance and lacks ear tufts. In this species the facial disc is rather indistinct, being pale grey with dark brown markings. The eyes are small and bright yellow and above them are two short, white eyebrow-like markings. The bill is pale yellow. Clad in off-white

Pygmy owl with dead mouse

feathering, the legs and feet of this owl are proportionately large
and robust, an adaptation which permits it to take vertebrate prey
up to its own size in weight. The tail is comparatively long and
barred with white and brown. In flight the pygmy owl can be seen
to have distinctly rounded wings. Upon landing it often cocks its
tail up sharply and when perched it has the habit of flicking its tail
sideways.

Little bigger than a chaffinch, the pygmy owl can be distinguished upon the basis of its small size alone. Only the scops owl of
southern Europe is a similar size and there is not a great deal of
overlap in the ranges of these two species. The scops owl is larger,
has small ear tufts and in contrast to the pygmy owl frequents open
areas with trees near human habitation.

Within Europe the pygmy owl is found in central and southern
Norway, central and southern Sweden, Finland, European
U.S.S.R. and mountainous regions of central and eastern Europe.
It is a sedentary species and only moves southwards from its

breeding range during severe winters. It occurs as a vagrant in Denmark, the Netherlands and Belgium but has never been recorded in Britain. Outside Europe the range of the pygmy owl extends across Asia, approximately between latitudes 50°N and 60°N but in the Far East its range extends southwards into parts of China. Two subspecies are recognized, that in Europe being *Glaucidium passerinum passerinum*, whereas the Far Eastern race is called *Glaucidium passerinum orientale*. In North America the Eurasian pygmy owl is replaced by a closely similar species, *Glaucidium gnoma* or northern pygmy owl.

Throughout its large range the pygmy owl is nowhere common, its habitat being extensive tracts of coniferous and montane forest away from human habitation. Birds living in the mountainous regions of central Europe will however move nearer to populated areas in winter when food is hard to find and also sometimes during summer when larger supplies of prey are required to satisfy the growing young.

The diet of this species consists very largely of small mammals such as voles, lemmings and mice. A variety of small birds are also taken on occasions, the pygmy owl being able to catch these in flight. Insects are also eaten when these are available during the summer months. There are records of pygmy owls storing food in tree cavities, presumably a consequence of superabundance.

The pygmy owl is partially diurnal, having flight feathers which lack sound-deadening filaments. Consequently it does not have the ability to fly silently and when hunting probably relies less upon hearing than do many other owl species. It frequently hunts by day when, like many small owl species, it shows little fear of man. However most activity takes place just before sunrise and shortly after sunset.

The pygmy owl is a distinctly vocal species as might be expected for a forest dwelling bird. Its call is heard most frequently during early spring at the start of the breeding season. This is a much repeated 'peeu-peeu-peeu'. It also utters a longer, whistling note which can be described as 'keeoo', and there is a 'kuvitt' call similar to that of the little owl.

The nest site is a tree cavity and the four to seven white eggs are usually laid during the first half of April. The incubation period is about four weeks and is said usually to begin when the third egg of the clutch is laid. The nestlings are at first clad in a whitish down but this is later replaced by the juvenile plumage. This is darker than that of mature birds with few pale markings on the upper-parts, and the under-parts are more heavily mottled with brown.

URAL OWL (*Strix uralensis*)

This is a large, generally light brown owl similar in appearance to its near relative, the much smaller tawny owl (*Strix aluco*). Its name is derived from the middle and south Ural mountains and the upper part of the Ural river which fall within its extensive range. The Ural owl is about 585 mm in length. The wings are proportionately quite long, the span being up to 1.2 metres. Females weigh 520 to 1,020 grammes and are on average heavier than the males which weigh 450 to 825 grammes. The plumage is generally a pale buff of either a greyish or brownish hue, streaked with dark brown. On the under-parts these streaks are long and pronounced. The wings and tail are transversely barred, the latter being quite long and well rounded. In spite of this brownish colouration, the Ural owl can appear distinctly whitish in flight. The facial disc is a uniform off-white and lacks any markings, a feature which contrasts with the concentrically lined face of the otherwise similar great grey owl (*Strix nebulosa*). Another difference between these two species are the eyes. The Ural owl has small dark brown eyes whereas the great grey owl has yellow eyes which are proportionately even smaller.

As with many owl species the range of the Ural owl is large. It is found from Scandinavia and eastern Europe in a band across Asia to Japan. The principal area in which this bird is resident in Europe includes Sweden, Finland, western U.S.S.R. and northern Poland with some birds in Norway. There is also a separate, scattered population in central Europe ranging through Austria, south-east Germany, southern Poland, Czechoslovakia, Romania, Yugoslavia and Albania. Interestingly, there is a similarly isolated population in western China. The Ural owl is normally sedentary but some birds wander outside their normal range during winter and in Europe this species has been recorded as a vagrant as far south as Italy. It is however unknown in Britain. As a result of this large and scattered range and the fact that Ural owls are sedentary by nature, there is a good deal of variation in the size and

Ural owlet

colouration of individuals from different localities. In consequence, about ten subspecies or races have been distinguished.

The Ural owl is a bird of coniferous and mixed forests and woodland. The population in central Europe is found at relatively high altitudes occupying montane forest in the Alps, the Carpathians, the Balkans and the Bohemian forest. In general, forest-edge and somewhat open areas are preferred. In winter the Ural owl will move nearer to inhabited areas such as farm buildings and the outskirts of villages in its search for rodent prey. The relatively small eyes of this species are testimony to its less strictly nocturnal habits as compared with other species such as the tawny owl. It hunts mainly during the hours of darkness but is also frequently active by day, although it is not as diurnal as the great grey owl.

The diet of the Ural owl is quite varied and unlike the great grey owl it is not a vole specialist, although these rodents do form a significant part of the diet. Larger mammals including the squirrel, weasel and hare are taken occasionally. A variety of birds such as woodpeckers, pigeons, thrushes, finches and jays are also eaten. Larger species recorded in the diet include the partridge, black grouse and hazel hen. Frogs, fish and beetles are also eaten on occasions. In order to deal with larger prey animals the Ural owl is equipped with relatively thick, strong claws.

There is a good deal of overlap in the ranges of the tawny owl and the Ural owl. Moreover these two species have similar requirements in terms of nest site and to a significant extent in diet. Consequently in areas where individuals of the two species coexist there may be competition between them for available resources and it is of interest to note that the Ural owl will kill and eat tawny owls that it encounters within its territory.

The onset of breeding is greatly influenced by the prevailing weather conditions in early spring and commences as soon as the snow has melted. Ural owls can be heard calling from late March, the hoot being a somewhat harsh 'huow-huow-huow'. There is also a call similar to, but again harsher and also longer than that of the tawny owl, best described as 'korrwick'.

In the north European population the nest is normally in a cavity in the broken trunk of a conifer; aged spruce and pine trees tend to break off three to six metres from the ground. Such sites are not too uncommon in mature forests but remain at a premium and it is for this reason that Ural owls are obliged to be sedentary in their habits. Movement during winter would mean loss of the nest site and Ural owls will often retain the same territory for life.

In northern Europe the eggs are laid in late April and early May but in the more southerly populations they may be laid up to a month earlier than this. There can be an interval of up to seven days between the laying of successive eggs. Normally three to four are produced but in years when food is either scarce or abundant the number may vary accordingly from two to six. Incubation is carried out by the female and requires about 28 days per egg. During the egg laying period males have been seen to present their mate with food, a piece of behaviour which may serve to strengthen the pair bond and which may also help to increase the egg laying capacity of the female.

From the clutch produced, normally only one or two young survive to the fledging stage, although occasionally three may do so. Fledging occurs after about 34 days in the nest. The Ural owl will fiercely defend its nest and will attack human intruders, sometimes inflicting serious injury.

Within northern Europe the Ural owl has shown changes in habitat and nest site preferences since about 1950 and in consequence its population size has increased. Areas of damp and dry heath forest and spruce bog are now inhabited and this species has become more tolerant of human habitations. Furthermore, since about 1960 Ural owls have begun to make use of nest-boxes where these have been provided.

GREAT GREY OWL (*Strix nebulosa*)

The great grey owl or Lapp owl is a very large greyish owl lacking ear tufts. In fact it is one of the biggest of the world's owl species, being 635 to 760 mm in length. Within this range the males are on average smaller than the females. Length however is not a very accurate indication of size as this species has a comparatively long tail. More significantly, beneath its deep plumage the great grey owl is a slim and lightly built bird, males weighing 700 to 800 grammes and females up to 1,200 grammes. In comparison the apparently similar sized eagle owl is a far more robust and heavier bird, weighing from 2 to 3.5 kg.

The upper-parts of the great grey owl are mottled and streaked grey, white and brown, the back of the head being barred with these colours. In flight a pale patch at the base of the primary feathers is evident and there are also white areas on the scapulars. The under-parts are white, heavily and broadly streaked and finely barred with grey-brown. The head is proportionately large and the eyes are yellow, a feature unique among the 11 species of the *Strix* genus. Furthermore the eyes of this partly diurnal owl are proportionately very small, being approximately 12.5 mm in diameter. In comparison, those of the closely related but very much smaller tawny owl are 16.5 mm in diameter. The eyes of the great grey owl are bordered with black feathering and between this and the yellowish bill there is on each side of the face a white, outwardly pointing crescent. There is also a small black area beneath the bill which is bordered on either side with white feathering. The remainder of the facial discs are white with seven or eight concentric circles of brown barring, this very distinctive face having a dark border. The great grey owl has broad, rounded wings. It flies with apparently slow wing-beats but is very agile when manoeuvring through trees.

There are two subspecies of this owl, that found in Europe and elsewhere in the Old World being slightly larger, paler, greyer and more finely marked below than its New World counterpart. The great grey owl is in fact the only member of the *Strix* genus to be found in the Nearctic. In Europe it is to be found in Finland, northern Sweden and Norway and northern parts of European U.S.S.R. The southernmost breeding site in Europe was once in the forest of Bielowicza, near Bialystok in eastern Poland, where this species last nested in 1955. From north-eastern Europe its range continues in a band across Asia approximately between latitudes 50°N and 65°N. It occurs as a vagrant in the more southerly parts of Norway and Sweden and also in Poland and Germany but it has never been recorded in Britain. In many parts of its extensive range the great grey owl is scarce or else its population size is liable to considerable fluctuation. In Finland for example, its numbers have been estimated to vary between 50 and 2,000 pairs as a direct consequence of variation in the numbers of voles. These changes are cyclical and relate to the production of cones by spruce, pine and larch which is at a maximum about once every three or four years. The abundance of seeds results in a vole 'plague' and in turn an increase in great grey and also hawk and Tengmalm's owls within the area concerned.

The great grey owl is a bird of dense, natural pine forest, although within this it seems to prefer areas where there are small stands of aspen, birch and other deciduous trees. However, it is rarely found in pure deciduous forest. Within this habitat it will hunt over open areas such as marshy land or sometimes birch scrub or heather heathland. When doing so, the great grey owl flies very low and close to the ground, dropping quickly upon any prey located. It is of necessity a partly diurnal species since its range extends far north into regions where there is perpetual daylight during summertime. Maximum activity is normally around early morning and late evening with the minimum amount of hunting taking place around midday and during the middle of the night.

In spite of its considerable size the great grey owl is very much a vole specialist in its diet and for this reason it has a light skeleton and long slender talons. In comparison, the eagle owl which generally feeds upon larger prey has much thicker and stronger claws. One study carried out in Sweden and Finland indicated that in summer the diet of the great grey owl consists of about 80 to 95 per cent voles with shrews comprising most of the remainder. A few rats and mice were also eaten. Remains of other species

Female great grey owl on nest

identified from the 4,000 pellets analysed were those of the mole, red squirrel, frog and a variety of small birds including waders, thrushes, finches and buntings. In winter, proportionately more shrews are eaten but voles are still the major item of diet at this time of year. There are a few records of larger prey being taken by the great grey owl on occasions, these including the blue hare, willow grouse and hazel hen.

The call of the great grey owl is a deep hoot which can be described as 'hoooooh hoooooh-hoooooh', the last syllable being longer and at a higher pitch than the first two. There is also a high pitched call very like the 'kewick' of the tawny owl. For such a large bird the voice is not particularly powerful, the call being said to carry no more than about 500 metres. During the breeding season this bird also makes a variety of barking, cooing and clicking calls. Surprisingly the breeding territory can be very small. From Sweden there is a record of two nests just 100 metres apart and in Finland three were once located within 400 metres of one another. It will tolerate within its territory other species of owl including the Ural, hawk and Tengmalm's owl.

The usual nest site is an abandoned nest of a bird of prey such as the goshawk, osprey or buzzard, usually in a pine, spruce or larch tree. Sometimes this nest is relined with a few leaves, pine needles or strips of bark. There are a few reports of the great grey owl constructing its own nest, these being flimsy twig platforms. It has never been known to nest in a tree cavity; this is perhaps a consequence of its relatively small eyes and presumably poorer vision in dim light when compared with other European owls.

As with all types of owl that rely heavily upon voles as a source of food, breeding performance in any one year is very dependent upon the population size of these rodents. Usually the clutch produced varies from two to six eggs but up to nine may be laid when prey is abundant. The eggs are laid between mid-April and mid-May and are white but more distinctly oval than those of most owls. The interval between the laying of each egg can vary from one to twelve days, so consequently there is sometimes a considerable difference in the age and size of the first and last chicks to hatch. Incubation takes about 28 days per egg and is probably always carried out by the female. At this time males have been observed to provide their mate with three or four voles or their equivalent per day, visits to the nest site normally being made during the darker hours. When half grown the young have mottled grey down and the developing facial discs are dark. Adult great grey owls will defend their nest vigorously against human intruders and are especially liable to be aggressive when the chicks are at about this stage of development. The young remain in the nest for a total of five weeks but after fledging they will stay in the vicinity of the nest and be dependent upon their parents for six to eight weeks. Furthermore, juvenile great grey owls have been known to stay within their parents' territory for several months before dispersing completely.

TENGMALM'S OWL (*Aegolius funereus*)

Tengmalm's owl inhabits coniferous forests in northern and central Europe. It is a small, brown owl about 255 mm in length and is thus similar in size to the little owl. However, with its proportionately large, round head and distinct facial disc, it is more like the larger tawny owl in outline. The upper-parts are a rich warm brown with distinct white spotting whilst the under-parts are grey buff and streaked with brown. The facial disc is generally pale grey in colour with a dark patch above each eye and broad, pale 'eyebrows'. It is surrounded by a pronounced brown and white ruff. The eyes are bright yellow and the bill a pale yellowish colour. Tengmalm's owl is able to raise some of its crown feathers at the front of its head, thus making it appear to have short horn-like tufts. The legs and feet are clad in pale feathering.

Tengmalm's owl can be distinguished from the little owl by a number of features. The latter is a dark brown colour with finer white streaking giving way to striations on the crown. In contrast, Tengmalm's owl has a crown spotted with white. Additionally, Tengmalm's owl has deeper facial discs which are not flattened above its eyes, testimony to its more nocturnal lifestyle when compared with the little owl. Other differences between these two species include the darker border which Tengmalm's owl has to its facial disc, its comparatively broad, white 'eyebrows', the presence of some barring on the under-parts and feathering on the toes. In general posture Tengmalm's owl is the more upright bird when perched, and its flight is reasonably direct and not undulating like that of the little owl. The only other European owl with which Tengmalm's owl may be confused is the smaller scops owl. One of the chief distinguishing features of the latter is the possession of small ear tufts.

Tengmalm's owl derives its name from Peter Gustavus Tengmalm, the Swedish ornithologist who first described this bird in 1783. In Sweden it is called *parluggla* which means 'pearl owl' referring to its distinct white markings. As for its scientific name, *Aegolius funereus*, the best translation is probably 'ill-boding owl'. *Aegolius* is derived from the Greek *aigolios* for a kind of owl and *funereus* is Latin for 'ill-boding'.

In Europe Tengmalm's owl is found in the Alps, the Jura and the Carpathians and it is found in lesser numbers southwards from these regions into the mountainous areas of the Balkans. Further north it is to be found in Germany, Poland and the forests of central and northern Scandinavia, and outside Europe its range extends eastwards across Asia in a band bordering on about latitude 65°N. A separate subspecies occurs in North America. Tengmalm's owl is normally sedentary but in winters when food is short it will wander outside its normal range and may occur as a vagrant in southern Scandinavia, Denmark and other European countries. The furthest south it has been recorded is Spain. It was formerly a more frequent visitor to Britain than during recent years. Prior to 1918 almost 50 of these birds were seen in Scotland and eastern England between October and February. More recent sightings include a bird which visited the Cruan Firth area in the Orkneys between 26 December 1959 and New Years Day 1960, and one seen in Stromness on 1 May 1961.

In northern Europe and the U.S.S.R. Tengmalm's owl is a bird of pine forest, but in central Europe it occurs in montane forest where it shows a preference for silver fir and birch trees. It is a nocturnal species but birds in the Arctic part of its range are obliged to hunt by daylight in summertime. Even so, in these areas it hunts largely around midnight when the sun is at its lowest. During the daytime Tengmalm's owl roosts in a conifer much in the manner of a long-eared or tawny owl, perched at the base of a branch, close against the trunk of the tree.

The diet of this owl consists principally of small mammals, mostly voles and lemmings but birds are also important and may comprise up to 40 per cent of the diet in some areas. Not surprisingly the species taken are usually small ones, for example tits and finches, but larger birds such as thrush species sometimes form part of the diet and there is a record of a rook being eaten by a Tengmalm's owl. Frogs are taken occasionally but insects seem to be eaten only rarely which is a distinct contrast to the diet of the little owl.

Being a relatively small bird, Tengmalm's owl has predators of its own to contend with, not least being some of the larger species of owl, including the eagle owl. It is also taken by diurnal birds of prey upon occasions, the goshawk for example. Its principal mammalian predator is probably the pine marten which will take incubating Tengmalm's owls from their nests.

This owl has a call of three to six rapidly repeated syllables which can be described as 'poo-poo-poo' and is not unlike the call of the hoopoe. It is normally the male which calls and usually he does so from a perch. Occasionally however the call is made while the bird is in flight when the last syllable is often accelerated into a trill. The call carries for a distance of up to 1.6 km and is more frequently heard in early spring as a prelude to the breeding season. Other calls include a barking 'kep-kep-kep' which is an alarm call made, for example, when the bird is disturbed at the nest.

The nest is always in a tree cavity, the abandoned nesting hole of a black woodpecker being preferred, but the holes of other, smaller species of woodpecker are sometimes used. No nesting material is employed, the eggs being laid on the bottom of the cavity. In the southern part of its range the first clutches are laid in mid March with the majority being produced in mid April. In more northerly

Young Tengmalm's owls at their nest in tree cavity

latitudes however it is quite usual for the eggs to be laid in May. The size of the clutch may vary from three to eight eggs, the largest on record being ten, these being glossy white and almost spherical. Incubation is carried out by the female alone and takes about 26 or 27 days. The young spend about five weeks in the nest and for the first three weeks they have a pale grey down. This is replaced by a distinct juvenile plumage which is sooty brown with a few white markings notably around the head. The fully grown young have a characteristic trilling call.

5 A comparison of lifestyles

It could be argued that the lifestyle of any species of bird is characterized principally by just three aspects: the nature of its diet, the type of nest site occupied and the habitat in which it lives. These factors are of course interrelated, for a bird must occupy a habitat which fulfils its needs for food and nesting. In the case of owls there is a fourth aspect of significance in their way of life, this being the time of day when they are normally active, for although the majority of owl species are nocturnal a substantial proportion are either partly or wholly diurnal.

If comparisons are made between the five species of owl widespread in Britain then it becomes apparent that no two are the same in all of these respects (Table 3). In fact it seems that each has a way of life which is unique and indeed the same probably holds true for all types of living organism coexisting in a particular area. This unique lifestyle of each species, or the place it occupies in nature, is more properly called its ecological niche. The value of this arrangement is that competition between closely related species for limited resources is reduced. For example, although the tawny owl and little owl may well coexist within an area, the former preys largely upon small mammals and birds whilst the latter eats mostly insects. Further, the little owl is often active by day unlike the strictly nocturnal tawny owl, so the two tend to hunt at different times of day.

One of the most interesting points evident from Table 3 is the difference in type of habitat occupied by each of the five species. Again this probably helps to reduce competition between them, but how is each type of owl confined within a particular type of habitat? Experiments carried out with the chipping sparrow (*Spizella passerina*) help to shed some light on this question. This North American bird normally lives in pine woods containing some deciduous trees. Within this habitat it shows a preference for

TABLE 3 SOME IMPORTANT ASPECTS OF THE LIVES OF BRITISH OWLS

Species	Habitat	Nest site	Diet	Period of Activity
Barn owl	Agricultural land, meadows, grassland	Lofts of outhouses and similar buildings. Sometimes tree cavities	Chiefly shrews, voles and rats	Normally nocturnal
Tawny owl	Deciduous and mixed woodland	Usually tree cavities	Varied. Chiefly small mammals with some invertebrates, notably earthworms	Normally nocturnal
Little owl	Well wooded farmland, parks and gardens. Mostly below 120 m altitude	Usually tree cavities	Chiefly insects and other invertebrates. Some small mammals	Often active by day. Hunts mainly at dawn and dusk
Long-eared owl	Mostly small woods, copses and plantations surrounded by open country	Abandoned nests of other species, e.g. magpie or crow. Usually in conifers	Short-tailed voles and other small mammals. Some birds	Strictly nocturnal
Short-eared owl	Open grassland and heath	Grassy hollows on ground	Chiefly short-tailed voles with some other small mammals and birds	Diurnal. Hunts mostly at dawn and dusk

97

pines. Wild, adult chipping sparrows were introduced into a large aviary containing pine trees at one end and oaks at the other. Not surprisingly these birds chose to occupy the area containing pines. In a second experiment a group of young chipping sparrows were reared from the time of hatching in the complete absence of foliage and then introduced into the experimental aviary at two months old. These birds chose to live in the pine area suggesting that habitat selection is instinctive and not a conscious choice based upon the birds memory of its surroundings during early life. In a further experiment young chipping sparrows reared in the presence of oak showed some tendency to occupy this type of tree. By the time they were one year old however, they had reverted fully to a preference for pine. Thus in chipping sparrows at least, habitat selection is largely under genetic control and visual experience at an early age seems to be unimportant in determining preference, but can modify it to some extent.

Whatever the mechanism involved, changes in habitat selection can and do occasionally occur and there are some interesting examples of this among owls. The association of barn owls with farmland and buildings is long-standing, but barn owls have been in existence for much longer than agricultural man. What then was their original habitat? More recently, tawny owls have colonized city parks and other similar areas, becoming much more tolerant of human presence. During this process their feeding habits have altered drastically, for the diet of woodland tawny owls consists of around 90 per cent mammals and 10 per cent birds, whereas in city-park owls these figures are approximately reversed. A recent and well documented change in habitats is that of the Ural owl in Finland. Since about 1950 this bird has begun to occupy areas of both damp and dry heath forest and spruce bog in addition to its original habitats of coniferous and mixed forest. It has also started to show an increasing tolerance of man.

Many species of owl have large geographical ranges and within these a good deal of variation exists in the type of habitat occupied. For example, in Britain the tawny owl is normally a bird of deciduous woodland but in many other parts of Europe coniferous forests are also inhabited and in some parts of northern Scotland it is found on open moorland where it nests on the ground. It would be of great interest to carry out experiments with tawny owls similar to those conducted with the chipping sparrow. In this way it may be possible to find out whether learning is of significance in determining habitat selection in the tawny owl or whether birds from different habitat types represent races with characteristic, instinctive behaviour patterns.

Of the factors important in the lifestyle of owls perhaps the most variable is diet. On the whole the diet of a particular species is fairly characteristic but a good deal of individual specialization exists suggesting that experience and learning play a greater role here than in habitat selection. Of possible relevance is the fact that young owls are dependent upon their parents for some time after fledging. During this period they may well be learning what to hunt as well as how to hunt.

Investigation of the diet of owls is comparatively easy because of course they regurgitate much of the indigestible remains of their prey in the form of pellets. These consist chiefly of bones, fur and feathers of vertebrates, together with the remains of invertebrates where these form part of the diet, for example worm chaetae and beetle wing cases. Pellets can be collected from the roost sites of individual owls at regular intervals and their contents analysed. Superficially this appears to be quite straightforward, the only practical problem to any systematic study being the fidelity of individual birds to their roost site. To some extent this varies between species; the barn owl for example will often occupy the same roost site regularly for months or even years whereas other species such as the short-eared owl tend to be more nomadic.

The aim of such studies is to determine the relative importance of different prey species in the diet but interpretation of the results has to be made with care. One of the chief problems is that not all prey animals are represented in regurgitated pellets because some are completely digested. In one experimental study involving captive tawny owls a careful record of the food intake was kept and all pellets analysed. It was found that about 85 per cent of the short-tailed voles eaten were represented by remains in the pellets whereas 67 per cent of bank voles, 60 per cent of wood mice and only 40 per cent of house mice were represented. Thus it seems that only a proportion of the prey taken by owls will be represented in their pellets and, more significantly, this proportion may vary between species. Consequently data obtained from pellet analysis may show a bias towards the less digestible prey species. Regrettably this problem has been little studied and it has generally not been taken into account in published works.

A further problem is that mere numbers of prey animals identified do not convey a very clear impression of their true importance in the diet for the simple reason that some prey species are much larger than others. For example, a pygmy shrew weighs as little as four grammes and a brown rat at least 100 grammes and often much more. A solution to this problem was devised by H. N. Southern and published in 1954 in connection with a study of the diet of tawny owls. In this case a 20 gramme rodent was taken as a standard and called one prey unit. A series of estimates were then made of the average weights of the various prey species, for example a brown rat was estimated to weigh 100 grammes and hence equivalent to five prey units. In comparison, one pygmy shrew comprised 0.2 prey units and a short-tailed vole one unit. Use of the prey unit system allows an estimate to be made of the percentage *by weight* of each species in the diet and hence their nutritional importance. This is achieved by converting the number of each species identified into prey units. Percentages are then calculated on the basis of the latter.

This prey unit system has been widely used but it does have certain limitations. For example a brown rat may weigh anything up to 500 grammes, equivalent to 25 prey units, a weight of 100 grammes being the estimated average of those taken which are in fact mostly young animals. In addition, all birds are assumed to weigh 20 grammes, regardless of species, so no distinction is made between, for example, a wren and a blackbird. Clearly in situations where birds form a significant part of the diet this method would not be satisfactory as it stands.

When studying the diet of owls a number of other factors have to be borne in mind. For any species, diet may vary between different geographical regions and between habitats. It may also vary with season and there could be differences in the diet of males, females and nestlings. Careful study can reveal such variation but combining data, for example from a variety of habitats, over a period of years will obscure any such details and provide a more general view. Some additional points to bear in mind are that prey may be shared by a family of owls during the breeding season and

Farm buildings are a typical barn owl nest site

some prey animals, especially large ones, may only be consumed partly and a proportion discarded.

In spite of these complexities the diets of British owls have been the subject of numerous studies. Table 4 is an attempt to summarize this information, but of course more data is available than can be satisfactorily tabulated in this manner.

One of the best studied of all the European owls is the barn owl and consequently a good deal is known about its feeding habits. In Britain the results of a large scale survey were published by D. E. Glue of the British Trust for Ornithology in 1974. This was based upon analysis of almost 50,000 pellets from 188 owls. It was found that shrews, voles, rats and mice made up most of the diet. In fact these species comprised about 90 per cent by weight of the vertebrates eaten, the remainder consisting of birds, bats, moles, rabbits, weasels and amphibians. Of the birds eaten by barn owls, house sparrows often predominated, but on average birds formed only two per cent by weight of the prey taken. Invertebrates were found to make up only a very minor part of the diet.

Interestingly, the prey taken by the barn owl appears to vary with habitat to some extent. The short-tailed vole is the chief prey species in Britain. Using Southern's prey unit system it was calculated that in areas of rough grassland this rodent makes up 75 per cent of the diet whereas in other habitats the proportion is generally lower. For example, in mixed farmland the figure is 50 per cent, in small grazing fields near woodland it is 30 per cent and

TABLE 4 THE DIETS OF BRITISH OWLS

OWL SPECIES	PREY SPECIES						NOTES
	Short-tailed vole	Other small mammals	Medium-sized mammals	Birds	Fish, amphibians, reptiles	Invertebrates	
Barn owl	About 50% varying with habitat	Common shrew 15%. Wood mouse 15%. Others recorded	Brown rat 10%. Others recorded	About 2%. House sparrow often predominates	Some amphibians taken	Very minor part of diet, chiefly beetles	Shrews and mice predominate in southern Europe
Tawny owl	About 15%	Wood mouse, bank vole and common shrew about 75%. Other recorded	Young rabbits, moles and brown rats can form 50% in summer	Normally about 5%. About 40 species recorded	Fish have been recorded	Can be significant. Chiefly beetles and earthworms.	Significant seasonal variation noted in Britain, see text
Little owl	Small part of diet	Small part of diet	Some young rats taken	Small numbers taken, more in breeding season	Lizards noted where available	Insects 50%. Slugs, snails and earthworms also important	—
Long-eared owl	About 40%, chief prey	Wood mouse 15%. Bank vole 10%	Brown rat 12%	About 10%, chiefly house sparrow and other small species	Reptiles and amphibians noted	Very small part of diet, chiefly beetles	—
Short-eared owl	Chief prey 50-85%	Wood mouse (more important in winter). Also bank vole and shrews	Brown rat, rabbit, water vole (all more important in winter)	More significant in winter, usually small species	—	Very small part of diet, chiefly beetles	Seasonal variation significant, see text

N.B. All figures are percentages by weight. They are inevitably approximations and the text should be referred to for further details.

in wet pasture and water meadows it is 50 to 75 per cent. In Ireland and on the Isle of Man the short-tailed vole and also the common shrew are absent. Here the chief prey species are the brown rat and the wood mouse.

A study carried out in Cumbria indicated some seasonal variation in the diet of barn owls. A total of 679 pellets were gathered from one roost over a period of two and a half years. Although a more limited investigation than that described above, the results are of interest. The two main prey were found to be the short-tailed vole and the common shrew which together formed almost 90 per cent of the diet. The other species of significance were the wood mouse and the pygmy shrew. The relative proportion of short-tailed voles eaten rose to a peak in autumn and winter whereas most common shrews were taken in spring and summer.

Elsewhere in northern Europe a similar dietary pattern seems to exist but further south the feeding habits of the barn owl differ. Investigations in Portugal, southern France, Greece and Crete have all shown that the house mouse forms 60 to 90 per cent of the diet and shrews make up a further 20 to 40 per cent. Here voles comprise less than 20 per cent of the food intake. In terms of numbers of species the diet of the barn owl is more diverse in southern Europe and it has been suggested that this is a result of the relatively sparse distribution of prey species.

The best known owl in Britain is arguably the tawny, and its diet shows some interesting differences from that of the barn owl. Like the barn owl it has been much studied, notably by H. N. Southern and others at Wytham Wood near Oxford. Here pellets were collected from the roosts of 20 pairs of tawny owls for a period of eight years, and this extensive study revealed a distinct seasonal variation in diet. From November to April small rodents were found to comprise 65 to 80 per cent of the prey, these being principally the wood mouse, the bank vole and the short-tailed vole. At this time larger prey such as moles, rabbits and brown rats made up about 15 to 25 per cent of the diet. From May to October the situation was quite different however with small rodents comprising only 30 to 45 per cent and larger mammals 45 to 60 per cent of the food. Other vertebrates such as shrews and small birds were found to be eaten regularly and in small quantities throughout the year. This seasonal variation seems to be connected with changes in vegetation during the course of the year, since small rodents are eaten in greatest numbers in late spring, before the ground becomes densely covered with grass and low herbage.

It seems likely that the comparatively early breeding season of the tawny owl is synchronized with these changes since by May the nestlings are already quite big and able to tackle larger prey. A significant proportion of the food brought to half grown tawny owls by their parents consists of young moles. Interestingly, beetles, especially cockchafers, are another important item of their diet. Unlike the tawny owl, barn owls and also the short-eared owl breed later in the year when the population density of their chief prey, the short-tailed vole, is at a maximum.

In contrast to the barn owl, invertebrates seem to form a larger proportion of the diet of the tawny owl. Studies at night using infra-red binoculars have revealed that tawny owls catch and eat many earthworms, and radio-tracking tawny owls in Sweden indicated that they spent much of their time walking through pasture fields when they were presumably hunting for earthworms and other invertebrates.

Studies in Britain and elsewhere in Europe have shown that the diet of the tawny owl varies a good deal with habitat and geographical location. One investigation in Belgium revealed a diet similar to that of the tawny owls in Wytham Wood but with less seasonal variation. Another study, carried out in Italy, revealed shrews to be the chief prey item. Elsewhere, birds have been shown to form a more significant proportion of the diet. In the Wytham Wood studies they comprised only about five per cent by weight of the diet but tawny owls occupying Holland Park in central London have been found to subsist very largely upon birds. Here the song thrush, blackbird and starling formed 37 per cent of the prey, the pigeon and jay 25 per cent and the house sparrow 31 per cent. Small mammals made up only seven per cent of the total. Similar findings have been noted in Germany where a large scale study carried out in the Grunewald pine forest of Berlin indicated a diet of 35 per cent birds, 29 per cent mice, 17 per cent voles and 13 per cent shrews. During winter the proportion of birds eaten rose to more than half. In a Berlin park, birds, chiefly house sparrows and greenfinches, were found to make up 70 per cent of the diet.

Typical short-eared owl habitat is this area of upland scrub and forestry plantations

In striking contrast to the diet of the barn and tawny owls is that of the little owl. Introduced into Britain at the end of the nineteenth century this bird became widespread in distribution by 1930. It was originally introduced because of its known value as a predator of mice and insect pests but later there were accusations of it taking large numbers of game and poultry chicks. It was also blamed for the decline in numbers of some wild birds. Consequently an investigation into its diet was organized by the British Trust for Ornithology, the results being published in 1936 and 1937. The study involved analysis of about 2,500 pellets and the stomach contents of 28 owls found dead. In addition prey remains were collected from 76 nest sites. Only seven pellets were found to contain the remains of poultry chicks and just two contained the bones of young game birds. In fact about half the diet of the little owl consists of insects, in particular earwigs, craneflies, moths and beetles, chiefly cockchafers. Slugs, snails and earthworms are also eaten, together with some voles, mice and young rats.

Britain's two other owls, the long-eared and short-eared owls show similarities to the barn owl in their feeding habits but as indicated in Table 4 they avoid competition to some extent by occupying different habitats and nest sites. The chief prey of the short-eared owl is the short tailed vole which is taken in the · greatest proportion during the summer months. One study showed that this species formed 83 per cent of the diet between

Ivy clad tree is a typical roosting site of long-eared owl

April and August whereas from September to March the proportion was only 50 per cent. The other significant prey animals noted were the wood mouse, the brown rat and a variety of small birds, all these being taken in greater proportions during the winter months. The diet of the short-eared owl is quite variable at this time of year; the dominant prey in certain areas studied included the brown rat in Norfolk and Cambridgeshire, the wood mouse in Yorkshire, the rabbit in Wiltshire and small birds in a number of other areas. Invertebrates, principally beetles, make up only a small proportion of the diet. Like the barn owl, different prey are taken in places where the short-tailed vole is absent, the chief species in Ireland and the Outer Hebrides being the brown rat and the pygmy shrew respectively.

Being heavily dependent upon the short-tailed vole as a source of food during spring and summer, the breeding performance of this owl can vary a good deal between successive years. This is because of large scale fluctuations in the population density of this rodent. Its numbers reach a peak about once every four years and then crash. In years when the short-tailed vole is abundant the short-eared owl will breed prolifically, and some examples of this are cited in the description of this species earlier.

The short-tailed vole is again the principal food of the long-eared owl although this bird is perhaps less of a vole specialist than the short-eared owl. In one large scale study in Britain, short-tailed voles were found to comprise about 40 per cent of the total prey weight. The other important prey species were the wood mouse (15 per cent), brown rat (13 per cent), bank vole (9 per cent) and birds (15 per cent), about half of which were house sparrows and the remainder chiefly finches, starlings, blackbirds and thrushes. Little seasonal variation in the diet of the long-eared owl was evident from this study although the proportion of birds taken was 8 per cent in spring and summer (March to July) and 23 per cent in autumn and winter (August to February). Again, in the absence of the short-tailed vole from Ireland there is an alternative staple food, in this case the wood mouse. Elsewhere in Europe the dietary pattern of this owl appears to be similar to that in Britain. Three independent studies carried out in northern Germany, southern Bavaria and south-eastern Hungary all found voles to be the chief prey species.

Regrettably the diets of some of the owl species inhabiting continental Europe have not been extensively studied. The available information is summarized in Table 5 and as might be expected there are some interesting comparisons to be made with the owls described above. The diets of two species are quite distinctive and reflect their geographical ranges to a large extent. These are the scops owl and the snowy owl.

The scops owl occurs in the southern half of Europe, south of about latitude 47°N. Its food appears to be almost entirely insects, especially beetles, moths, grasshoppers and crickets with some small mammals and birds being taken occasionally. Being principally insectivorous, it is perhaps not surprising that the scops owl is a partial migrant, moving southwards to winter in the Mediterranean region and in central Africa.

The snowy owl is of course a bird of northern tundra regions having a circumpolar distribution. Its chief prey is the lemming and where these rodents do not occur it is either rare, as for example in Iceland, or else it is absent altogether as on Jan Mayen and Franz Josef Land. Assuming that an average lemming weighs

TABLE 5 THE DIETS OF EUROPEAN OWLS

OWL SPECIES	PREY SPECIES					NOTES
	Small mammals	Medium-sized mammals	Birds	Fish, amphibians and reptiles	Invertebrates	
Scops owl	A few mice and shrews taken occasionally	—	A few eaten	—	Diet almost entirely insects, chiefly moths, beetles and grasshoppers	—
Eagle owl	Some taken, e.g. voles and lemmings	Hedgehog, young hare and brown rat often chief prey	Wide variety of medium-sized species important	Amphibians and fish can be important	—	Diet is varied. See text for examples
Snowy owl	Almost all of diet is lemmings. Some voles taken, notably in winter	Arctic hares eaten on occasions, more so in winter	Can form part of diet, e.g. waders	Fish taken occasionally, e.g. charr	—	—
Hawk owl	Voles are chief prey, especially in summer. Some lemmings eaten, especially in winter	—	More important in winter, e.g. willow grouse and ptarmigan	—	—	—
Pygmy owl	Voles form about 50% of diet. A few mice and shrews also eaten	—	Small species form up to 50% of diet	Lizards noted on occasions	A few insects taken in summer	Young birds are one of chief foods of nestlings
Ural owl	Short-tailed and bank voles are chief prey	Of some importance, e.g. water vole, red squirrel and young hares	Small and medium-sized species, e.g. partridge and hazel hen	Amphibians and fish taken on occasions	A few beetles are eaten	Young fed extensively on water voles
Great grey owl	Voles form 80–95% of diet, shrews forming most of remainder	Eaten occasionally, e.g. brown rat, mole, red squirrel	Small species taken occasionally, e.g. thrushes and finches	Frogs noted in diet	—	—
Tengmalm's owl	Diet is chiefly voles and also lemmings	—	Up to 40% of diet in some areas, e.g. tits and finches	Frogs eaten on occasions	Rarely eaten	—

108

60 grammes, it has been calculated that the minimum number a snowy owl must eat in order to survive a sub-artic winter is four a day. Observation of snowy owls on Baffin Island, Canada, during the breeding season revealed that at this time of year the adults eat three to five lemmings per day. In addition each nestling is on average provided with two fully grown lemmings every 24 hours. As is well known, the population density of lemmings is highly variable. In fact it reaches a maximum about every four years when the celebrated migrations take place. For the snowy owls in the area concerned, the autumn following such a migration is not surprisingly a period of hardship. At such times they rely more heavily upon other prey such as voles and arctic hares and also move southwards in larger numbers than is usual. In normal years some snowy owls winter in the breeding grounds, often subsisting upon arctic hare and ptarmigan in addition to lemmings.

The diets of the other three large European owls have been studied in some detail. It might be expected that these species take comparatively bigger prey and this is certainly true of the eagle owl. Two independent studies in the Bavarian region indicate that the hedgehog, young hares and the brown rat are the most significant prey species, particularly during the breeding season. In one of the studies these three species comprised more than 50 per cent by weight of the food. Medium-sized birds were also found to be taken, including partridges, carrion crows, feral doves, mallard and long-eared owls. Overall the diet of the eagle owl is diverse and does include both small mammals such as voles, lemmings and mice, and occasionally larger species such as the wild cat. There is a good deal of variation in diet between geographical areas, between successive years in the same area and even between individuals. In one area of the Carpathians where the small mammal population is particularly inclined to fluctuate considerably, about 30 per cent of the diet comprises frogs and toads. In some areas, birds are a significant part of the diet, for example in Sweden where they were found to constitute 33 per cent of the food with mammals making up 55 per cent and, interestingly, fish a further 11 per cent. The population of eagle owls in western Norway relies heavily upon birds as a source of food; these make up 83 per cent of the diet. Half of these are sea birds, principally the common gull, eider duck and puffin. The full list of avian prey is lengthy, ranging in size from the thrush to the great black-backed gull and the capercaille, and includes a range of diurnal birds of prey such as the rough-legged buzzard, sparrow-hawk and peregrine falcon. Even large, young white-tailed eagles are sometimes taken from their eyries. In some areas of Norway up to 36 per cent of the diet is estimated to be birds of prey.

The eagle owl appears to be intolerant of the presence of other owl species within its territory and removes at least some individuals by predation. Those taken include the long-eared owl, tawny owl, little owl, Tengmalm's owl, hawk owl and even the snowy owl.

The diets of the two large *Strix* owls of Europe are in marked contrast to that of the eagle owl. The overall prey spectra of the great grey owl, the Ural owl and the tawny owl are similar, more especially those of the latter two species. The chief prey animals of the Ural owl are the short-tailed and bank voles but compared with the tawny owl there is a greater emphasis upon medium-sized mammals and birds such as the water vole, partridge and hazel hen. In addition, one study revealed that the bulk of the food brought to half-grown nestlings consists of water voles (more than 65 per cent by weight of the total). Apart from dietry similarities, the Ural and tawny owls both nest in tree cavities, so there does appear to be some competition between them. This may be reduced to some extent by the fact that the Ural owl will sometimes hunt in daylight, unlike the strictly nocturnal tawny owl. Nevertheless where their ranges overlap the latter does fall prey to the larger Ural owl.

The great grey owl is the most diurnal of the three European *Strix* species and in spite of its considerable size it is very much a vole specialist. A number of studies in Sweden and Finland indicate that these rodents make up 80 to 95 per cent of the diet and shrews comprise most of the remainder. In winter proportionately more shrews are eaten but voles remain the major source of food. In further contrast to the tawny and Ural owls it does not nest in tree cavities but takes over the abandoned nests of birds such as the osprey, goshawk or buzzard. The great grey owl is known to tolerate the presence of the smaller tawny owl within its territory, perhaps because there is evidently not much competition between them.

In continental Europe it seems possible that at least two other species might come into competition with the *Strix* owls to some extent, these being the long-eared owl and Tengmalm's owl. Both feed largely on voles and competition for these must become especially acute in winter when their numbers are at a minimum and they can take refuge beneath a covering of snow. One option for the owls is to disperse or migrate south in winter but there are conflicting pressures for some species. In Scandinavia and Finland the Ural owl and tawny owl are resident throughout the year, partly because they are more general feeders and turn to alternative prey during winter. More significantly they nest in tree cavities which are scarce commodities and, it seems, too valuable to abandon every autumn. Pairs of Ural owls are in fact faithful to their territories for life.

In contrast, Scandinavian and Finnish long-eared owls are migratory. Leaving their breeding territories is not a problem since they use old nests of other species and these are never in short supply. For Tengmalm's owl however there is an interesting conflict. On the one hand it feeds largely upon voles so migration is desirable, but on the other it nests in tree cavities. As a compromise in this part of its range the males remain within their territories all year round but the females and young birds are migratory. Apart from voles, Tengmalm's owl feeds extensively upon lemmings. Birds can form up to 40 per cent of the diet in some areas but insects are taken only rarely.

Europe's smallest owl, the pygmy owl, is also a hole-nesting species and largely resident. Although substantial proportions of voles are eaten, birds can again form a significant part of the diet, at least during the breeding season, and the pygmy owl is able to catch these in flight. In one study carried out in southern Finland the spring and summer diet consisted of voles (50 per cent) and birds (44.5 per cent), the remainder being small numbers of shrews, mice, bats, lizards and insects. In this part of its range the pygmy owl breeds comparatively late in spring, probably so that the nestling stage is timed to coincide with the abundance of young birds which one of the chief food sources. In comparison, another investigation carried out in the Bayerischer Wald National Park in West Germany revealed a breeding season diet of 76.5 per cent mammals with the proportion of birds varying from 10.3 to 36.7 per cent between years.

The last remaining European owl species to be mentioned is the hawk owl, a diurnal bird of northern Europe which nests in tree cavities. As might be expected from this it tends to be sedentary except when food is particularly scarce. In summer its diet largely consists of voles, with lemmings, small birds and insects taken only occasionally. In winter however its feeding habits become much more diverse and in one study voles were found to make up only about 40 per cent of the food intake and birds some 33 per cent. Among the latter, willow grouse are important and there are records of hawk owls following flocks of these birds, and also ptarmigan, during periods of deep snow when mammalian prey is especially difficult to locate.

In conclusion an attempt has been made to summarize the lifestyles of the owls of continental Europe in Table 6. This is similar to Table 3 which deals with the British species. There are of course other aspects to the ecology of owls than those described above but regrettably many of these are poorly understood at present. Owls for example have their own predators, especially the smaller species such as Tengmalm's owl, females of which can fall prey to the pine marten (*Martes martes*) during the incubation period. Other carnivorous animals such as the wild cat (*Felis silvestris*) are known to take owls occasionally, although here the tables can be turned for there are records of wild cats in the diet of eagle owls. Smaller species of owl are eaten by larger ones, chief among the latter in this respect being the eagle owl, as noted previously. Among other examples, bones of the long-eared owl have been found in the pellets of the slightly larger tawny owl. This is interesting because in Ireland, where the tawny owl is absent, the long-eared owl is relatively numerous and in Northumberland, the Lake District and the Wigtown area the tawny owl has increased in numbers whereas the long-eared owl has declined. Thus in spite of the fact that each species of owl seems to be uniquely fitted to a particular way of life there appears to be at least some competition between species for food and living space. In addition, owls must at times come in to competition with carnivorous mammals. For example in British woodlands the tawny owl is said to compete with the weasel (*Mustela nivalis*) for food, the diet of both species including voles, rats, mice and moles.

Lastly, some comment on the influence of man on the ecology of

TABLE 6 SOME IMPORTANT ASPECTS OF THE LIVES OF EUROPEAN OWLS

Species	Habitat	Nest Site	Diet	Period of Activity
Scops owl	Gardens, orchards, parks and hedgerows with trees	Usually tree cavity	Almost entirely insects	Nocturnal
Eagle owl	Open woodland in mountainous areas to 4,500 m	Usually shallow depression on ground	Diverse. Chiefly medium-sized birds and mammals	Nocturnal, hunting mostly at dawn and dusk
Snowy owl	Tundra regions	On ground, favouring rocky outcrops	Almost entirely lemmings. Some voles and arctic hares in winter	Diurnal
Hawk owl	Thinly wooded areas, e.g. forest clearings	Usually tree cavity	Mostly voles with a few lemmings, birds and insects. Birds more important in winter	Diurnal
Pygmy owl	Large coniferous and montane forests	Tree cavity	Chiefly voles and small birds	Partly diurnal
Ural owl	Chiefly coniferous and mixed forest and woodland	Tree cavity, e.g. broken conifer trunk	Short-tailed and bank voles. Also medium-sized mammals and birds	Generally nocturnal. Sometimes active by day
Great grey owl	Dense natural pine forest	Abandoned nest of bird of prey, e.g. buzzard	Very largely short-tailed voles. The remainder chiefly shrews	Partly diurnal. Hunts mostly during early morning and late evening
Tengmalm's owl	Coniferous and montane forest	Tree cavity	Chiefly voles and lemmings. Birds sometimes important	Nocturnal

owls should be made. It is probably fair to state that man has significantly influenced the numbers and distribution of some species of owl but that he does not affect their lifestyle. The felling of woodland and establishment of arable farmland probably favoured the barn owl at the expense of the tawny owl. The slow but progressive decline in numbers of the barn owl and the long-eared owl in Britain is probably a consequence of the intensification of agriculture. In this way man may provide or remove suitable territories, nest sites and even food species and so affect population levels of owls, but he does not affect for example the time of day when an owl species normally hunts or what species it normally chooses to prey upon.

To define success with respect to animal species in the natural world is not easy but however one tries to do this, the owls as a group must surely be among the most successful of birds. With about 135 living species they do not form a large order but several species such as the barn owl have a worldwide distribution and their global populations must be very great. In Britain the most numerous owl is the tawny with an estimated population of about 100,000 individuals. Owls are undoubtedly very specialized birds, nocturnal hunters *par excellence*, but a high degree of specialization can be a disadvantage for it can lead to extinction if the environmental conditions the species requires alter or disappear. Owls however are very adaptable birds as evidenced for example by the subtle interplay of dietary, territorial and migratory strategies described earlier for some of the owl populations of northern Europe. Moreover some species of owl are able to survive and flourish in environments greatly altered by man, notably the tawny owls of city centre parks in many parts of Europe.

Perhaps one of the ultimate tests of success is the test of time and here again the record of the owls is impressive. Many of the present species and genera are of great antiquity, the genus *Asio* taking pride of place, having been in existence for at least 36 million years. In attempting to speculate about their future, with the exception of the possible effects of man, it is difficult to see how these birds could lose their grip on the spectrum of ecological niches over which they hold a worldwide monopoly and for which they are supremely well adapted.

6 Owl watching

The obvious beginning to the study of any species of bird is of course to look for it in a suitable place and some indication of the habitats occupied by owls is provided in Tables 3 and 6. Since many owl species are nocturnal one might think that they are not easy birds to find and observe but this habit at least means they are generally static during the day which helps when first trying to locate them. By day woodland species such as the tawny and long-eared owls roost on tree branches, often close to the trunk. Here they are very well camouflaged and one can often walk several times around a known roosting tree and fail to spot an owl, knowing full well that one is almost certainly present. Tawny owls will roost in evergreens such as yew or holly, in ivy clad trees or others providing good cover.

A careful inspection of the ground beneath a possible roost site is always worthwhile. Regurgitated pellets may be found, these being a sure sign that the tree has been occupied recently. The persistent alarm calls of small birds such as thrushes, finches and tits are another tell-tale sign. This mobbing behaviour can often be directed towards another species such as a kestrel or jay but the bird concerned is frequently an owl discovered at its roost by one of the mobbers. Although the mobbing birds are quite conspicuous the owl may be hard to spot unless it tries to avoid harassment by taking to the air in search of an alternative roost.

At night the tawny and long-eared owls can be located by their calls as this is when they are most active. They are especially vocal during autumn when territories are established and early in the year during courtship. A red torch can be used to observe owls at night since like many nocturnal animals their eyes are not sensitive to this colour. Britain's other nocturnal owl, the barn owl, often roosts and nests in the lofts of barns and out-buildings. Perhaps the best way to find this species is to ask the owners of likely buildings for information and permission to visit known roosts.

The short-eared and little owls are more diurnal species and to some extent they are easier to observe. However this is only true of the former during the breeding season when it is tied to its nest site which is usually on open ground. During winter the short-eared owl is quite nomadic and several of these birds might be seen at a particular spot on one day and by the next they may well be gone. Although no bigger than a song thrush the little owl is quite bold and unafraid of intruders. If approached with a little caution it will often oblige by remaining at its perch, staring inquisitively at the observer.

A time of year of special interest to many bird-watchers is the breeding season. However several points need to be borne in mind before setting out to observe owls at this time. Firstly, some species will often vigorously defend their nest site and the immediate vicinity by attacking an intruder. There have been cases of severe facial injury to people approaching nests of the *Strix* owls, that is the tawny, Ural and great grey owls. It is strongly recommended that anyone wishing to approach the nests of these species for the first time should do so in the company of a suitably experienced person. A second point to be borne in mind is that in many countries owls are afforded legal protection and this may well include their nest sites. In Britain for example the snowy and barn owls are Schedule One species, meaning that it is an offence to disturb them at the nest. Observers, notably those wishing to take photographs, must obtain the permission of the Nature Conservancy Council before approaching the nest sites of these species. Considering its rarity, one can appreciate why there is special legislation to cover the snowy owl in Britain. Also the barn owl is known to be slowly but steadily declining in numbers, but the same is true of the long-eared owl and yet it is not a Schedule One species. However, the latter together with the tawny owl, short-eared owl and little owl, is covered by the Protection of Birds Act 1954–67 which means that it is an offence to wilfully kill or injure these birds, to take them into captivity or to take or damage their nests or eggs.

Whatever the legal position, all those with a genuine concern for wild birds would put the interests of an owl before their own observations and care must be taken accordingly when near a nest site. It is quite possible to observe the nest site of, for example, a tawny owl without causing disturbance by approaching no closer than about 25 metres. If one arrives before sunset and before the birds become active it is possible to sit or stand behind a suitably positioned tree trunk and simply watch from there.

The more ambitious observer can construct a hide. Here, obtaining the practical assistance of an expert is perhaps the best course of action but in any event certain guidelines should always be followed. Firstly, the hide should be built a distance of about 25 metres from the nest site and then gradually moved nearer, only a few yards each day, in order to allow the birds to become accustomed to its presence. Such a hide can be made from green or brown canvas or other suitable material secured to an internal frame and camouflaged with local vegetation. No part of the structure should be free to blow about in the wind since this could cause disturbance. The time spent building should be no more than 15 minutes per day and it should be done around noon when the birds are least active. Hide construction should never be carried out during the incubation period since disturbance at this time could cause the female to desert the nest. Of course some pairs of owls nest quite high in trees and a hide placed in a nearby tree or a tall framework may be desired. In this case expert advice and help should be sought in order to ensure that the hide is safe and that its construction does not worry the birds. When approaching a hide it is important to have someone accompany the observer. This person should then leave as the observer quietly enters the hide. Most birds, including owls, are unable to count, so by doing this they will be led to think that the hide is not occupied and moreover they will not learn to associate it with the presence of people.

Compared with woodland owls, barn owls are less difficult to observe at their nests since, when occupying a building, they generally pay little attention to reasonably quiet humans. Again care should be taken to keep away from the nest until incubation has been completed. In a place such as a dark loft it is possible to use a dull red torch as this will not disturb the birds.

For the owl watcher there is much of interest to be seen during the nestling period. In the case of the tawny owl and many other species, when bringing prey to the nest the male always uses one particular landing perch in a nearby tree. He then calls to the female, in the tawny owl this being the 'ke-wick' call. When the young are small or if the weather is cold the male will take the food to the nest. When the young are larger the female will leave the nest to collect prey from the male. Finally when the nestlings are well grown the female will leave them and join the hunt for food. By careful observation of a nest, the nature and numbers of prey species provided for the young can be recorded. There is much scope for making original contributions to the knowledge of breeding in owls since many aspects do not seem to have been widely studied. For example there are very few published descriptions of courtship display in most owl species. The effect of adverse weather upon the success of hunting and the consequent development of offspring is poorly understood. In tawny owls at least, there are reports of males storing excess prey items in the vicinity of the nest site, sometimes in old crows' nests. Whether this is exceptional behaviour or quite usual is unknown. Male tawny owls often have favourite vantage points from which they hunt but it would be interesting to know just what makes a suitable hunting site, how many a particular owl may have and how much it relies on them as opposed to less habitual ways of hunting. Reliance upon hunting stations may or may not vary with season, weather conditions or the abundance of particular prey species.

Once young owls have left the nest they will remain in their parents' territory for several weeks. Remember that young owls are at first very poor flyers and it should not be assumed they have fallen from their nest by accident, and consequently they should not be handled in any way. The following are examples of what can and has been learnt from the careful study of fledged tawny owls. These observations were made by H. N. Southern and others at Wytham Wood near Oxford. Firstly it was found that survival of young owls through this period was surprisingly high. Over a period of three breeding seasons the progress of 71 fledglings was followed from mid May until mid August. Of these only two could not be located by the end of July. Interestingly, the young owls did not feed themselves during this period and relied entirely on their parents for food. Two quite distinctive juvenile calls were noted and described as 'ke-serp' and 'ke-suip', the former being lower pitched. It was found that individual birds only ever used one of these calls. In situations where just one owlet from a brood survived to fledging it uttered only one or the other of these two

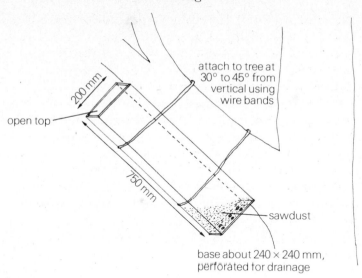

Fig 13. Tawny owl nest-box constructed from wood about 20 mm thick and coated with yacht varnish. Cleaned out and revarnished annually, this should last many years

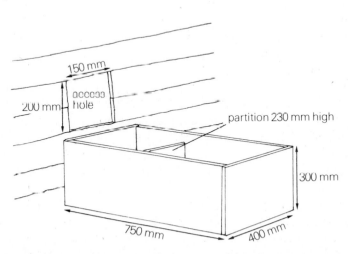

Fig 14. Barn owl nest box constructed from wood about 10 mm thick and sited in a loft or outbuilding. The birds should nest in the part furthest from the access hole. The other part provides space in which the adults can deposit prey for the young

calls. In broods of two, one fledgling used one of these calls and the second bird the other. Just one brood of three fledglings was studied and here the ratio of call types was two to one. It seems possible that these call differences may help the parents recognize each of their offspring when they are out of sight.

Should the opportunity provide itself, several owl species will take to nest-boxes and some suitable designs are shown in Figures 13 and 14. These are not very difficult or costly to make and allow the possibility of having an owl family in a known and convenient place to observe. In addition, nest-boxes are of great benefit in areas where natural nest sites are in short supply. Any information gathered by observers about the breeding performance of owls would be of value to the British Trust for Ornithology (Tring, Hertfordshire, England) for the Nest Record Scheme (Mayer-Gross, 1972).

A quite different area offering major scope for the individual bird-watcher is the study of owl diets via the analysis of pellets. Once seen for the first time these are not too difficult to locate in the field. They form because the gastric juice of owls is not very acidic, and bone and other hard substances are not readily dissolved. Also, the opening from the stomach to the intestines is comparatively small in owls. Consequently the only way in which such remains can be voided is by regurgitation.

Pellets of the tawny owl are usually of a crumbly texture and grey in colour. They are about 30 to 70 mm in length and 20 to 25 mm in diameter. The place to look for them is beneath likely roosting trees. Indeed their presence is a valuable guide to which trees are currently being occupied. Pellets produced by the long-eared owl are similar in size and appearance and may of course be found in similar woodland habitats. Obviously care should be taken to ascertain which species has produced any pellets collected. Pellets of the little owl are comparatively small, usually being 30 to 40 mm long and 10 to 15 mm in diameter. Those of the barn owl are quite distinctive, being black and glossy. They are about the same size as those of the tawny owl. Since barn owls are often faithful to a roost for many months or even years, systematic collection of their pellets is comparatively easy. Pellets of the short-eared owl are about 35 to 70 mm long and 15 to 25 mm in diameter. They are usually compact, dark grey in colour and characteristically deposited in the open grassland habitats occupied by this owl.

If desired, pellets can be stored by placing them in suitable containers with mothballs to prevent decay. Analysis can be carried out in one of two main ways. Pellets can be teased apart while dry, using forceps. Alternatively they can be fragmented by boiling with a trace of washing soda for a few minutes. Following this, most hair and feathers will float and most bones should sink. The former can then be poured off. Although not necessary, bones can be bleached with a solution of 20 volume hydrogen peroxide and an equal amount of water to which a trace of ammonia is added. Finally they should be washed and dried.

The most useful remains for identifying mammals are skulls and lower jaws, whereas for birds the pelvis (synsacrum), breast bone and leg bones are of particular value. Some excellent guides to the identification of mammalian skulls exist, notably that of D. W. Yalden (Yalden, 1977). Regrettably there do not seem to be any such works dealing with birds. Perhaps the best long-term solution to the problem of identification is to build up a reference collection of skeletons. If the corpse of any small mammal or bird found dead is buried in soil for a period of about six months the soft parts of the body will rot away entirely. When investigating pellets it is always worthwhile looking out for the more unusual items such as the remains of amphibians and reptiles, fish scales, wing cases of beetles and the bristles of earthworms. The presence of vegetation, sand or soil in a pellet will suggest that the owl has been eating earthworms or possibly caterpillars.

A good deal has been said about the interpretation of data gained from pellet analysis in the previous chapter. Little can be added except perhaps to say that D. W. Yalden (Yalden, 1977) has produced a useful method for estimating the weight of a bird from the length of its humerus. This can be used even if the species is unknown and so the method is of great help in estimating the nutritional significance of birds in the diets of owls.

In conclusion it can be said that as with all aspects of natural history there is nothing more satisfying and enjoyable than first hand experience of this unique and fascinating group of birds. It is hoped that although brief, the above shows just how much scope exists for the observation and practical study of owls.

Bibliography

GENERAL TEXTS

BURTON, J. A. (ed.) (1980) *Owls of the World* 2nd edn. Eurobook, London

COWARD, T. A. (1964) *The birds of the British Isles and their eggs* 7th edn. Warne, London

EVERETT, M. (1977) *Natural history of owls* Hamlyn, London

GEROUDET, P. (1965) *Les rapaces diurnes et nocturnes d'Europe* Delachaux et Niestle, Neuchatel

SPARKS, J. and SOPER, T. (1977) *Owls: their natural and unnatural history* 2nd edn. David and Charles, Newton Abbot

WITHERBY, H. F., JOURDAIN, F. C. R., TICEHURST, N. F. and TUCKER, B. W. (1940) *The handbook of British birds* Witherby, London

SELECTED PAPERS AND OTHER WORKS

ANDERSSON, M. and NORBERG, R. A. (1981) 'Evolution of reversed sexual size dimorphism and role partitioning among predatory birds.' *Biol. J. Linn. Soc. (Lond.)* 15, 105–130

BEVEN, G. (1964) 'The food of tawny owls in London.' *London Bird Report* 29, 56–72

BEVEN, G. (1970) 'Tawny owl' in J. Gooders (ed.), *Birds of the world* (IPC, London) 4, 1340–44

BEWICK, T. (1976) *Selections from History of British Birds* Paddington, London

BEZZEL, E. (1972) 'Some notes on the food of the long-eared owl (*Asio otus*) in southern Bavaria.' *Anz. Orn. Ges. Bayern* 11, 181–4

BEZZEL, E. et al. (1976) 'On the diet of the eagle owl (*Bubo bubo*).' *J. Orn. Lpz.* 117, 210–38

BRDICKA, I. (1970) 'Eurasian eagle owl' in J. Gooders (ed.), *Birds of the world* (IPC, London) 4, 1314–16

BROCK, J. (1970) 'Eurasian pygmy owl' in J. Gooders (ed.), *Birds of the world* (IPC, London) 4, 1329–30

BROCK, J. (1970) 'Tengmalm's owl' in J. Gooders (ed.), *Birds of the world* (IPC, London) 5, 1365–7

BRUNO, U. (1973) 'Observations on the biology of the little owl (*Athene noctua*).' *Anz. Orn. Ges. Bayern* 12, 163–75

BUCKLEY, J. (1976) 'Barn owl (*Tyto alba alba*) pellets from Portugal.' *Bol. Soc. Port. Cienc. Nat.* 16, 133–6

BURTON, J. A. (1970) 'Little owl' in J. Gooders (ed.), *Birds of the world* (IPC, London) 4, 1336–9

CHEYLAN, G. (1976) 'The diet of the barn owl *Tyto alba* in the Mediterranean zone.' *Terre Vie* 30, 565–79

CURTIS, W. E. (1952) 'Quantitative studies of the vision of owls.' Ph.D. Thesis, University of Cornell, USA

DE BRUIJN, O. (1979) 'Feeding ecology of the barn owl, *Tyto alba*, in the Netherlands.' *Limosa* 52, 91–154

DEGN, H. J. (1976) 'An analysis of pellets from the long-eared owl (*Asio otus* L.) in Funen.' *Flora Fauna (Stockh.)* 82, 59–64

DELAMEE, E. et al. (1979) 'Comparative study of a feeding regime of a forest population of tawny owls (*Strix aluco*).' *Gerfaut* 69, 45–78

EVERETT, M. and SHARROCK, J. T. R. (1980) 'The European Atlas: Owls.' *Br. Birds* 73, 239–56

FERGUSON-LEES, I. J. (1970) 'Eurasian scops owl' in J. Gooders (ed.), *Birds of the world* (IPC, London) 4, 1303–6

FERGUSON-LEES, I. J. (1970) 'Ural owl' in J. Gooders (ed.), *Birds of the world* (IPC, London) 5, 1347–9

FERGUSON-LEES, I. J. (1970) 'Great grey owl' in J. Gooders (ed.), *Birds of the world* (IPC, London) 5, 1352–7

FLEGG, J. J. M. (1970) 'Long-eared owl' in J. Gooders (ed.), *Birds of the world* (IPC, London) 5, 1357–61

FLEGG, J. J. M. and GLUE, D. E. (1971) *Nestboxes, Field Guide No. 3* British Trust for Ornithology, Tring

FOERSTEL, A. (1977) 'The eagle owl *Bubo bubo* in the Franconian Forest and in the Bavarian Vogtland (Upper Saxonian Saale).' *Anz. Orn. Ges. Bayern* 16, 115–32

GLUE, D. E. (1967) 'Prey taken by the barn owl in England and Wales.' *Bird Study* 14, 169–83

GLUE, D. E. (1970) 'Owl pellets' in J. Gooders (ed.), *Birds of the world* (IPC, London) 5, 1368–70

GLUE, D. E. (1974) 'Food of the barn owl in Britain and Ireland.' *Bird Study* 21, 200–210

GLUE, D. E. (1977) 'Feeding ecology of the short-eared owl in Britain and Ireland.' *Bird Study* 24, 70–8

GLUE, D. E. (1977) 'Breeding biology of long-eared owls.' *Br. Birds* 70, 318–31

GLUE, D. E. and HAMMOND, G. J. (1974) 'Feeding ecology of the long-eared owl in Britain and Ireland.' *Br. Birds* 67, 361–9

GLUE, D. E. and SCOTT, D. (1980) 'Breeding biology of the little owl.' *Br. Birds* 73, 167–80

HARRISON, C. J. O. and WALKER, C. A. (1975) 'The Bradycnemidae, a new family of owls from the Upper Cretaceous of Romania.' *Palaeontology* 18, 563–70

HARRISON, J. (1970) 'Snowy Owl' in J. Gooders (ed.), *Birds of the world* (IPC, London) 4, 1322–6

HERRERA, C. M. (1974) 'Trophic diversity of the barn owl *Tyto alba* in continental western Europe.' *Ornis. Scand.* 5, 181–91

HIBBERT-WARE, A. (1937). 'Report of the little owl food enquiry 1936–7.' *Br. Birds* 31, 162–264

HOLMBERG, T. (1976) 'Variation in prey selection by the tawny owl (*Strix aluco*).' *Flora Fauna (Stockh.)* 71, 97–107

JOHANSEN, H. (1978) 'Nest site selection by the Ural owl.' *Flora Fauna (Stockh.)* 73, 207–10

KELLOMAKI, E. (1977) 'Food of the pygmy owl *Glaucidium passerinum* in the breeding season.' *Ornis. Fenn.* 54, 1–29

KLOPFER, P. and HAILMAN, J. P. (1965) 'Habitat selection in birds.' *Advances in the Study of Behavior* ed. Lehrman, D. S., Hinde, R. A. and Shaw, E., 279–303, Academic Press, New York

KNOETZSCH, G. (1978) 'Colonization experiments and notes on the biology of the little owl (*Athene noctua*).' *Vogelwelt* 99, 41–54

KNUDSEN, E. I. (1981) 'The hearing of the barn owl.' *Scient. Am.* 245, 83–91

LUNDBERG, A. (1976) 'Breeding success and prey availability in a Ural owl *Strix uralensis* Pall. population in central Sweden.' *Zoon.* 4, 65–72

LUNDBERG, A. (1979) 'Residency, migration and a compromise. Adaptations to nest site scarcity and food specialization in three Fennoscandian owl species.' *Oecologia* 41, 273–82

MACDONALD, A. W. (1976) 'Nocturnal observations of tawny owls *Strix aluco* preying upon earthworms.' *Ibis* 118, 579–80

MAYER-GROSS, H. (1972) *The nest record scheme, Field Guide No. 12*, 2nd edn. British Trust for Ornithology, Tring

MEAD, C. (1970) 'Short-eared owl' in J. Gooders (ed.), *Birds of the world* (IPC, London) 5, 1362–5

MIKKOLA, H. (1976) 'Owls killing and killed by other raptors in Europe.' *Br. Birds* 69, 144–54

MUIR, R. C. (1954) 'Calling and feeding rates of fledged tawny owls.' *Bird Study* 1, 111–17

NILSSON, I. N. (1977) 'Hunting methods and habitat utilization of two tawny owls (*Strix aluco* L.).' *Fauna Flora (Stockh.)* 72, 156–63

NORBERG, R. A. (1976) 'Occurrence and independent evolution of bilateral ear asymmetry in owls and implications in owl taxonomy.' *Phil. Trans. R. Soc. Ser. B* 280, 375–408

NORBERG, R. A. (1978) 'Skull asymmetry, ear structure and function and auditory localization in Tengmalm's owl, *Aegolius funereus* Linn.' *Phil. Trans. R. Soc. Ser. B* 282, 325–410

O'NEILL, J. P. and GRAVES, G. R. (1977) 'A new genus and species of owl (Aves, Strigiformes) from Peru.' *Auk* 94, 409–16

PARSLOW, J. (1970) 'Hawk owl' in J. Gooders (ed.), *Birds of the world* (IPC, London) 4, 1327–9

PAYNE, R. S. (1962) 'How the barn owl locates its prey by hearing.' *Living Bird* 1, 151–89

PRESTT, I. (1970) 'Barn owl' in J. Gooders (ed.), *Birds of the world* (IPC, London) 4, 1295–1300

PULLIAINEN, E. and KALEVI, L. (1977) 'Breeding biology and food of the great grey owl, *Strix nebulosa*, in a north eastern Finnish Forest, Lapland.' *Aquilo. Ser. Zool.* 17, 23–33

REISE, D. (1972) 'Investigations on the dynamics of small mammal populations. Pellet analysis.' *Z. Saugetierk* 37, 65–7

SCHERZINGER, W. (1974) 'The juvenile development of the eagle owl (*Bubo bubo*) compared with that of the snowy owl and short-eared owl.' *Bonn. Zool. Beitr.* 25, 123–47

SCHERZINGER, W. (1974) 'Study on the ecology of the pygmy owl *Glaucidium passerinum* in the Bayerischer Wald National Park.' *Anz. Orn. Ges. Bayern* 13, 121–56

SCHMIDT, E. (1973) 'The food of the barn owl (*Tyto alba*) in Europe.' *Z. agnew. Zool.* 60, 43–70

SCHMIDT, E. (1975) 'Quantitative investigations on small mammal remains in pellets of the long-eared owl.' *Vertebr. Hung.* 16, 77–84

SHALTER, M. D. and SCHLEIDT, W. M. (1977) 'The ability of barn owls *Tyto alba* to discriminate and localize avian alarm calls.' *Ibis* 119, 22–7

SHARROCK, J. T. R. and SHARROCK, E. M. (1976) *Rare birds in Britain and Ireland* Poyser, London

SOUTHERN, H. N. (1954) 'Tawny owls and their prey.' *Ibis* 96, 384–410

SOUTHERN, H. N. (1969) 'Prey taken by tawny owls during the breeding season.' *Ibis* 111, 293–9

SOUTHERN, H. N. et al. (1954) 'The behaviour of young tawny owls after fledging.' *Bird Study* 1, 101–10

VAN DIJK, T. (1973) 'A comparative study of hearing in owls of the family Strigidae.' *Neth. J. Zool.* 23, 131–67

VICKERS, R. P. and BOHASKA, D. J. (1976) 'The worlds' oldest owl: A new strigiform from the Palaeocene of southwestern Colorado.' *Smithsonian Contrib. Palaeobiol.* 27, 87–93

WATSON, A. (1957) 'The behaviour, breeding and food ecology of the snowy owl *Nyctea scandiaca*.' *Ibis* 99, 419–62

WENDLAND, V. (1972) 'Fourteen years observations on the reproduction of a tawny owl (*Strix aluco* L.) population.' *J. Ornithol.* 113, 276–86

WESKE, J. S. and TERBORGH, J. W. (1981) '*Otus marshalli*, a new species of screech owl from Peru.' *Auk* 98, 1–7

YALDEN, D. W. (1977) *Identification of remains in owl pellets* Mammal Society, Reading

Index

Picture credits

Black and white
A. Wardhaugh: p.28
A. Anderson/NHPA: p.9
D. Smith/Nature Photographers; pp.20,87,91
D. Smith/Aquila: p.62
G. F. Date/Aquila: p.45
N. W. Harwood/Aquila: p.47
C. K. Mylne/Nature Photographers: p.51
Dr. K. J. Carlson: pp.56,67,71,
P. D. V. Weaving/Aquila: p.72
A. Molinier/Jacana: p.75
E. Murtoäaki/NHPA: p.78
P. Helo/Bruce Coleman: p.81
N. Olsen/Aquila: p.84
H. Reinhard/Bruce Coleman: p.95
R. T. Mills/Aquila: pp.101,105,106

Colour
E. K. Thompson/Nature Photographers: no.1
E. K. Thompson/Aquila: no.6
W. Walter/Aquila: no.2
Harfang/Jacana: no.3
Brian Hawkes: no.4
J. Jeffrey/NHPA: no.5
J. Lawton Roberts/Aquila: no.7
F. Blackburn/Nature Photographers: no.8
Photo Library International – Leeds: no.9
H. Reinhard/Bruce Coleman: nos.10,13,16
B. Paton/Nature Photographers: no.11
W. Lankinen/Aquila: nos.12,15
D. Smith/Nature Photographers: no.14